THE GREAT WAR
10
CONTESTED QUESTIONS

THE GREAT WAR

10 CONTESTED QUESTIONS

Based on ABC RN's special broadcast
Foreword by Geraldine Doogue

ABC
Books

The ABC 'Wave' device is a trademark of the
Australian Broadcasting Corporation and is used
under licence by HarperCollins*Publishers* Australia.

First published in Australia in 2015
by HarperCollins*Publishers* Australia Pty Limited
ABN 36 009 913 517
harpercollins.com.au

HarperCollins*Publishers*
Level 13, 201 Elizabeth Street, Sydney, NSW 2000, Australia
Unit D1, 63 Apollo Drive, Rosedale, Auckland 0632, New Zealand
A 53, Sector 57, Noida, UP, India
1 London Bridge Street, London, SE1 9GF, United Kingdom
2 Bloor Street East, 20th floor, Toronto, Ontario M4W 1A8, Canada
195 Broadway, New York NY 10007, USA

ISBN 978 0 7333 3417 7 (paperback)
ISBN 978 1 4607 0488 2 (ebook)

Content based on the RN broadcast *The Great War: Memory, Perceptions and
10 Contested Questions*, produced by Annabelle Quince and Gary Bryson
Cover design and illustration: Design by Committee
Typeset by Kirby Jones in Adobe Caslon Pro
Printed and bound in Australia by Griffin Press
The papers used by HarperCollins in the manufacture of this book are
a natural, recyclable product made from wood grown in sustainable
plantation forests. The fibre source and manufacturing processes meet
recognised international environmental standards, and carry certification.

CONTENTS

FOREWORD

by Geraldine Doogue

Australians used to be taught that the causes and conduct of World War I were relatively easy to understand. In 1914 Germany and its allies wanted war and forced Britain and France to fight. But the politicians and generals on both sides did not grasp what they were starting, and within weeks technology overwhelmed tactics. The result was four years of senseless slaughter, which started for the Anzacs at Gallipoli and ended in France when the British, with Australians in the forefront, finally defeated the German army.

Certainly these easy ideas are true but the course of World War I did not travel along a single straight line. Rather, there are innumerable interconnecting ideas and events, creating a Gordian knot of actions and alternative outcomes. The retrospective narrative of war, all wars, assembled for the survivors and their children, is almost certainly absurdly simplified: a key insight for me after the RN program *The Great War: Memory, Perceptions and 10 Contested Questions*, on which this book is based.

As the historians who discuss the war in this series show, reducing the conflict to a single, simple timeline somehow assumes that all shared the same range of experiences. But nothing could be further from the truth. The digger at Anzac Cove bore his own horrors, which were different to the Indian cavalryman's in France; the woman working in a munitions factory in England might well have grieved the loss of friends and brothers alongside tens of millions of parents from Marseilles to Moscow, Berlin to Boston, but maybe none of them could properly articulate why their sons died in foreign fields.

The historians who talk in this series also provide a powerful antidote to the hubris of the present that leads us to assume the war was just a catastrophic diversion on the road to where we are today: wiser, richer and facing infinitely more complex challenges and risks.

In fact, what we learn from historian Margaret MacMillan is that the world in 1914 was shaped by threats and opportunities resulting from greed and hope, fear and arrogance as complex as those the world faces today in the Middle East and Ukraine, Africa and on the South China Sea.

We learn that Europe and some of its offspring states, notably Australia and New Zealand, Canada and the United States, were rich and growing richer, as their economics interconnected, peoples migrated and cultures exchanged. In 1900 the British were as friendly and familiar with Germans as they were with their "American cousins". And yet in the decade before the war, optimism was tempered by blights of racism and militarism — in France and Germany just about every man of military age had served in the army and knew that they could be called up to fight if one of the regular crises over colonies in Africa were not settled.

War was not inevitable as we were once taught. Historian A.J.P. Taylor's famous phrase "war by timetable" convinced the '60s generations that Europe blundered into war as the plans that generals drew up to defeat the enemy in a single enormous battle failed. Historians now recognise that the generals and ministers, especially politicians in all the great European capitals in the summer of 1914, made mistakes born of anger and error, and miscalculated, in other words, what friends and foes would do. Australian historian Christopher Clark suggests the statesmen walked the warpath together but this does not mean there were not alternatives.

Who led the march to war is still important, and not just to scholars. In Germany the question of responsibility for the First World War is tied up with guilt over the Second. The 50-year struggle of German scholars to explain whether the vain and impetuous Kaiser pushed Europe into the abyss is a revelation.

And when the war came it changed the world in a way then unimaginable to the people of Europe, America and Australia. In 1914 the last great conflict, the American Civil War, was a half-century in the past. The most recent major struggle in Europe, the Franco-Prussian War, was 40 years prior.

And as the war that was supposed to be over by Christmas in 1914 continued for three more, nearly reaching a fourth, it brought concentrated slaughter on a scale previously unknown in human history. Some 22 million soldiers were killed and wounded in World War I — over half the total forces. But was the war longer and bloodier than it should have been because soldiers were, as historians argued in the '60s, "lions led by donkeys"? This is still debated — some scholars argue that even in the democracies people were prepared to accept death on a scale that no government today would dare permit. And so generals, most infamously British commander Douglas Haig, were profligate with the lives of millions of men.

Others point out that the commanders had to learn the awful art of trench warfare by trial and terrible error, and that it was not until the middle of 1918 that the British and their allies, notably Australian commander John Monash, learned how men could cross machine-gun swept ground, capture enemy trenches and break through into open country.

What is not debated is the suffering of the wounded, many of whose bodies and minds were broken by the war, and whose experience was described by poets who shaped our understanding of it, notably Siegfried Sassoon and Wilfred Owen. The literature of the war marks what was perhaps the "end of Christian Europe", as centuries of popular religion were reduced to ashes by the grinding battles of 1916 and 1917.

But the poetry of the war we have read focused on the front in France, which makes it too easy to ignore that

World War I was just that — a global conflict. The stories of the Canadians and New Zealanders and white South Africans who fought are similar to our own. But the way we still focus on these soldiers means we miss the way the British enlisted Indians and Africans and the French enlisted those from their Vietnamese colonies. And the focus on the trenches of Flanders and France ignores the way the conflict was a truly world war — also fought in Eastern Europe and Africa, in the Middle East and on the oceans of the world as the Royal Navy pursued first German commerce raiders and then the U-boats which came close to closing Great Britain's Atlantic life-line.

In the end, World War I poses a paradox and a conundrum, both unresolved a century on.

The paradox is that the war the poets described and the historians analyse was, and is, essentially an affair of elites. Yet it was a people's struggle, where the beliefs and values of the men in the trenches and the women in the fields and factories were universally tested and found wanting. Religion, patriotism, hope for the future could not explain what was occurring.

The epitaph on the headstone of a soldier from Sydney, William Rae, who died in 1918 at Villers Bretonneux in France, captures this conundrum. "Another life lost, hearts broken, for what", his parents Arthur and Annie asked. It is a question that is still unanswered. Yes the war stopped Germany's king acting on his ambitions for empire but it did not prevent a German dictator trying again 20 years later. And the world is still paying the price for the colonial settlement in Africa and the Middle East. But while it is not possible to calculate the benefit, this series shows the cost. World War I was not the war to end all wars those who fought it hoped for — but it should have been.

1

THE CONTESTED BEGINNING

What really caused the war?

*The lamps are going out all over Europe. We shall not
see them lit again in our lifetime.*

— Sir Edward Grey, British Foreign Secretary, 3 August 1914

How can the cause of World War I be a contested
question? Just ask any high-school history student
and they'll tell you it began because of the June 1914
assassination of Austria's Archduke Franz Ferdinand by
Bosnian Serb nationalist Gavrilo Princip.

That act was indeed the trigger, the excuse, for the war
that Austria-Hungary declared four weeks later against
Serbia. But what turned this localised Balkans crisis into

a black hole that dragged in most of Europe and brought death and destruction on an unprecedented global scale?

Looking back, knowing the end-point as we do, we think we see an inexorable series of linked steps leading to war. But that's an illusion of hindsight. Even as that tense European summer unfolded and alliances between various nations pushed and pulled them into place on opposing sides, the outcome was far from a certainty. World War I was not inevitable and it did not have something everyone can agree on as its cause. The reality was much more nuanced and complex.

But the myriad of factors that led to war is not the only reason we're still debating the question of what caused the conflict — and who should be blamed — 100 years later. The passage of time also influences us. Each generation sees World War I through the prism of its own experience; the state of the world now influences how we interpret the state of the world then.

Let's start, then, with the context, including the scale of change the Europeans of 1914 had witnessed in their lifetimes. Professor Margaret MacMillan, author of *The War that Ended Peace: The Road to 1914*, notes that over those decades Europe had become a great industrial power. Its people had seen "the growth of cities. They'd seen the spread of communications, the spread of greater participation in government." These were sweeping developments that brought real and significant change to the lives of ordinary people. It was "the reform of society: the creation of jobs, adequate health care, votes for all," adds historian Paul Ham, whose books include *1914: The Year the World Ended.*

For many — though not all — the beginning of what we now called globalisation was deeply unsettling. With investment, trade and travellers flowing more freely across borders, people feared for their cherished national identities and sovereignty. "One of the reactions to rapid globalisation is to take refuge in small identities," says MacMillan, "and so you see in the period before 1914 a growth of nationalism: Scottish nationalism, Welsh nationalism, Irish nationalism."

Discontent grew among those who had begun to see themselves as cogs in a vast wealth-producing machine. Millions turned to socialism, believing it offered a fairer future. Others were united by special interests such as the push for colonial acquisition, particularly in Germany.

Germany had only unified as a nation (under Prussian force) in 1871. It was more than two centuries behind Britain's march across the globe. The new entity was fighting to establish its own empire in distant lands, including New Guinea and the Solomon Islands archipelago, to which Britain and the Netherlands also laid claim. It became, says MacMillan, "a great national cause: Germany must have one or two Solomon Islands". To the colonial lobbyists, expansion was imperative.

Also from within Germany came pressure to radically build up its navy, rather than focusing on its army as it had to date. Britain viewed naval strength and superiority as vital to its own security and answered Germany's naval build-up with its own, a race that MacMillan describes as "very, very destructive".

Military build-up in various European countries was strenuously supported by those who believed that a long period of peace had made their nations weak and unprepared. According to Ham, "Many senior Prussians, Germans, British and French believed that war was simply part of the natural order of things." MacMillan says that this sector felt that "military virtues — the ability to sacrifice yourself for a cause, the ability to accept discipline, bravery, and so on" were lacking in civilian society. "They felt that young people needed to be toughened up and that civilian society needed to be imbued with military values." Others came at it from a slightly different angle, she says, seeing war as something that could "paper over the divisions in society".

But there were diametrically opposing views from the huge and active peace movements forming throughout Europe. In looking at conflicts such as the Franco-Prussian War of the 1870s, these people saw something that belonged to the past; something they thought civilisation had outgrown. In addition, there were huge numbers who weren't part of a formal movement but shared those peaceful ideals; millions of what Ham calls "unasked people who didn't want to go to war; who would have liked to have seen society develop and evolve as it had been doing so well and so prosperously up until 1914".

There was much to encourage those who favoured peace: in the preceding years diplomatic effort had prevented numerous disputes between nations from flaring up further. For much of the 19th century, in what became known as "the Concert of Europe", Russia, France, Austria-Hungary, Britain and Germany had collectively worked to try to keep the peace, with much success. Even when war threatened they were mostly able to pull back from the brink, although in some cases grievances and rivalries lingered on.

In 1898, for instance, British and French troops faced off over territory in the Sudan but tempers cooled and battle was avoided. By 1904 the two countries had reached a diplomatic agreement called the Entente Cordiale — a political solution to their competing colonial interests — which in essence gave Britain free run in Egypt in exchange for letting France do as it wished in Algeria and Morocco.

The following year, unhappy with this cosy deal, the German emperor, Wilhelm II, sailed to Morocco and declared his support for the country and its sultan. This provoked major international consternation and became known as the First Moroccan Crisis. But France, England and Germany were able to resolve it around the negotiation table. In 1911 French troops entered Morocco and Germany sent a gunboat in response; this was the Second Moroccan Crisis. But again, diplomacy saved the day.

As late as 1912 and 1913 the First and Second Balkan Wars saw fighting between five countries and fatally weakened the Ottoman Empire in Europe, yet neither war spread because the competing claims were negotiated at peace conferences. Given this recent history, Paul Ham says, the conflict in 1914 initially was seen by some as a third Balkan war, which could have been contained.

Of course, it didn't play out that way. Those in charge, dynastic leaders still convinced of the divine right of royalty to rule, were determined to maintain control over increasingly restive populations. "Huge democratic pressures and political pressures were threatening and making the rulers of Europe apprehensive," says Ham. "In various regimes you had a cauldron of social pressures building up, which these very un-democratic regimes were determined to crush."

Facing outward against a perceived threat was the most effective way of bringing internal critics to heel. By presenting their own country as the aggrieved party, these leaders could draw together disparate and competing groups into one united force. As Ham says, "The extreme and often violent nationalism that we saw in the first decade of the 20th century became a far more powerful social glue than reform. When we think of World War I people often say, 'They were fighting for four years over a line on the map.' Well, they weren't. They were fighting for four years for the survival of their regimes, their dynasties, centuries of inherited wealth and power."

As summer began in 1914 Europe was basically divided into two camps, explains Dr Annika Mombauer, author of *The Origins of the First World War: Controversies and Consensus*. On one side was the dual alliance between Germany and Austria-Hungary, which were closely tied and had a firm commitment to support one another's interests. They were also in a triple alliance with Italy, but this was a much looser arrangement.

The other camp consisted of France, Britain and Russia, with ties between them of varying strengths. The alliance between France and Russia was firm. But, Mombauer says, rather than being known as a triple alliance, the arrangement is usually referred to as "the triple Entente" because Britain had not signed a formal alliance agreement: "This becomes important during the so-called July Crisis of 1914 because Britain can, in a sense, choose whether or not to become involved in a way that France and Russia can't, and Germany and Austria-Hungary on the other side can't. They are committed to supporting each other."

There is, however, a crucial caveat in even the tightest of these alliances. Should there be war, it must be justifiable; partners are not obliged to support one another in a war of aggression. This caveat would assume huge importance in the days and weeks following Franz Ferdinand's assassination, when each of the main players would take pains to appear the aggrieved party, being forced into war to defend itself.

There were two reasons behind the assassination: it was a protest over Austria-Hungary's designs on the Balkans and a show of support for Serbia. Princip lived in Sarajevo, the capital of Bosnia-Herzegovina, which for 40 years had enjoyed some self-rule despite being firmly a part of the Austro-Hungarian Empire. But then in 1908 the empire suddenly annexed it and took total control. This, says Mombauer, was regarded as an affront by a number of countries, particularly neighbouring Serbia. The First and Second Balkan Wars had seen Serbia expand considerably, but its ambitions were not yet satisfied. There were many ethnic Serbs living in Bosnia, and Serbia wanted to unite them in a greater Serbia. Austria-Hungary saw this as a threat to its very existence.

Tensions were already high when Princip left home and made his way to the Serbian capital, Belgrade. Here he was indoctrinated and trained by the group Union or

Death, better known as "Black Hand", led by the head of Serbian military intelligence. Princip and six fellow young would-be assassins were equipped with bombs and guns and smuggled over the border into Bosnia in time for an official visit by Franz Ferdinand, heir to the Austrian throne, and his wife, Sophie.

Details of the three-day visit had long been known and the route the couple would take in an open car on 28 June was advertised, allowing Black Hand members to position themselves strategically. Warnings about security were ignored and, astonishingly, the Archduke had insisted on proceeding with the afternoon's program despite a narrow escape earlier in the day when one of Princip's group had lobbed a bomb at the royals' car only to have it bounce off.

An unfortunate wrong turn by the royals' driver followed by a pause to reverse put the couple and their assassin in fatal proximity. Princip shot both of them point blank. These murders were shocking — the equivalent, perhaps, of a radical Australian group killing Britain's Prince William and his wife on a state visit. Princip's action was "an example of cross-border terrorism and an infringement of state sovereignty," says Professor John

Langdon, author of *July 1914: The Long Debate 1918–1990*. "That resonates today."

But as outrageous as the killings were, they still might not have led to war. The weeks after the shootings were filled with frantic attempts to shore up support on behalf of countries inclined to war and equally strenuous attempts by many, including British Foreign Secretary Sir Edward Grey, to prevent it. This was the July Crisis.

Finally, on 23 July, almost a month after the events in Sarajevo, Austro-Hungarian Minister Baron Wladimir Giesl delivered an ultimatum to the Serbian government, giving it 48 hours to react. Serbia was never supposed to meet the demands; Austria-Hungary had decided this was the trigger it needed for a war intended to crush Serbia. As Mombauer has noted, Giesl's official instructions were, "However the Serbs react to the ultimatum, you must break off relations and it must come to war."

Professor Michael Neiberg, author of *Dance of the Furies: Europe and the Outbreak of World War I*, has observed that we refer to this period as the July Crisis, not the June Crisis: it wasn't the assassination itself that destabilised Europe, it was Austria-Hungary's response to it. "The Austrian intellectual Stefan Zweig was right,

I think, when he said 'only a few weeks more and the name and figure of Franz Ferdinand would have disappeared for all time out of history',” says Neiberg.

Margaret MacMillan says that Austria-Hungary knew Russia might come to Serbia's defence, but pursued its reckless path anyway. Its leaders were emboldened by the response they had received in Berlin in the days after the assassination. “The German government gave what came to be known as 'the blank cheque' … They said, 'Do what you want. We will back you.' And that's what really turned what was a minor crisis in the Balkans into something much, much more dangerous.”

But, Mombauer has written, “the Serbian response to the 'unacceptable' ultimatum astonished everyone and has generally been regarded as a brilliant diplomatic move. The Belgrade government agreed to most of the demands, making Austria's predetermined decision to reject Belgrade's response look suspicious in the eyes of those European powers who wanted to try to preserve the peace.”

Pressure was building on Britain to make its position clear: would it step up in support of its Entente partners or remain neutral? Sir Edward Grey was preoccupied by the question of Irish independence, but even so he tried repeatedly, in vain, to get the various parties in the July Crisis around a conference table. At the very last minute the German chancellor proposed a non-military solution. But it was too little, far too late.

Britain delayed declaring its position as long as possible; torn, writes Mombauer, between the consequences of either a German or Russian victory. "It would have had grave consequences for Britain if Russia had managed to win the war without British support. But if Germany had won, Britain would have faced a Germany-dominated Europe."

France had its firm commitment to support Russia … but only as long as Russia went to war defensively, not as an aggressor. Russia itself was shocked at Austria-Hungary's tactics and regarded its demands as "wholly unacceptable to the Kingdom of Serbia as a sovereign state". On 26 July the Russian army began mobilising — something that would see war guilt attributed to it in later years. But Russia, presenting its mobilisation as a worst-case measure, continued to support Grey's efforts and urged Serbia not to resist armed invasion should it happen.

Even after Austria-Hungary declared war on Serbia on 28 July, Russian ruler Tsar Nicholas II reached out to Germany's Kaiser Wilhelm II — his first cousin. At 1am on 29 July Nicholas ("Nicky") sent a telegram to Wilhelm ("Willy") that read in part, "An ignoble war has been declared to a weak country … To try and avoid such a calamity as a European war I beg you in the name of our old friendship to do what you can to stop your allies from going too far." Wilhelm replied saying he shared Nicholas's wish for peace but felt Austria was justified. He suggested Russia could "remain a spectator of the Austro-Serbian conflict without involving Europe in the most horrible war she ever witnessed."

On 31 July Wilhelm wrote, "I now receive authentic news of serious preparations for war on my eastern frontier. Responsibility for the safety of my empire forces preventive measures of defence upon me. In my endeavours to maintain the peace of the world I have gone to the utmost limit possible. The responsibility for the disaster which is now threatening the whole civilised world will not be laid at my door." He told Nicholas war could still be avoided if Russia halted its mobilisation.

From Russia Nicholas replied, "It is technically impossible to stop our military preparations which were obligatory owing to Austria's mobilisation. We are far from wishing war. As long as the negotiations with Austria on Serbia's account are taking place my troops shall not make any provocative action." The following day Germany declared war on Russia. The dominoes fell. On 2 August Germany invaded neutral Luxembourg and two days later moved into Belgium. At this, Britain declared war on Germany. World War I had begun.

As unlikely as it might seem now, each participant continued to maintain that their actions were defensive, "even if, in the case of Germany, that defence requires an offensive action against Luxembourg and Belgium," says Mombauer. "This is obviously an easier argument for Belgium to make than it is for Germany, but nobody in Germany in 1914 thinks that this is a war of aggression. In Germany, they think it's started by Russia and France. In France they think it's started by Germany and Austria-Hungary, and so on." This perception is crucial, she adds, not just to secure back-up from alliance partners but also to win over the people, including those millions belonging to socialist movements: "the workers who had said they were not going to be involved in a war".

Fighting had barely begun before the scramble started to allocate (and avoid) blame for the war. "In 1914–1915 governments around Europe published selections of papers to show that they were innocent and others were guilty," says MacMillan. After the war the desire to sheet home responsibility became acute. By then there was also a practical aspect to it — the question of who should provide recompense for the damage done. Germany was, MacMillan notes, the only one of the defeated nations "still in any condition to pay".

Blame was codified in the Treaty of Versailles, signed at the 1919 peace conference. It was spelled out in article 231, which came to be known in Germany as "the war guilt clause". As John Langdon explains, the clause stated that "the Allied and associated parties affirmed and Germany accepted sole responsibility for the outbreak of war." Germany's partner Austria-Hungary would have been in there too, but the Austro-Hungarian government no longer existed after the war.

The primary reason for the clause was to justify the collection of reparations from Germany. But not only did Germany not accept that it was responsible for starting the war, it didn't even accept that it had lost it — after all, it held more territory when the war ended than when it had begun. Indeed, says Langdon, German Chancellor

Philipp Scheidemann resigned rather than lend validity to article 231. "He said, 'If I sign the treaty, my hand would wither.'"

The problem, says Langdon, was that the clause assigned *all* the guilt to Germany, rather than distributing responsibility among a number of powers but placing *most* of it on Germany and Austria-Hungary. This caused huge uproar in Germany. "Arguably it is one of the reasons why Hitler and the National Socialists managed to become so successful," says Mombauer, "because this opposition to the Treaty of Versailles, to the war guilt question, unites an otherwise politically completely divided Weimar Germany. That's the one thing that pretty much everyone can agree on." Adds Langdon, "As Hitler himself said in the early 1930s as he was poised to come to power, 'If the Versailles Treaty had not existed, it would have been necessary for us to invent it.'"

Margaret MacMillan points out that lessons learned from the First World War were applied at the conclusion of the Second. "The Allies said, 'OK, this time we're having no if and buts about who lost. We want unconditional surrender on the part of those who are our enemies.'" It worked. "Have we ever heard since the end of the Second World War that it really wasn't the fault of Germany, Japan, or Italy? We never hear that."

But at the end of World War I questions of blame lingered. In Germany, says Mombauer, successive governments made it their mission to demonstrate that the Treaty of Versailles was unfair, setting up journals, funding historians and censoring those who disagreed.

Throughout the 1920s and '30s various governments released documents dating from the July Crisis and before. "We're talking about tens of millions of pages that were suddenly declassified then dumped on the world," says Langdon. "This caused tremendous controversy because various historians and journalists and politicians sifted through this mass of evidence and picked documents that, to a greater or lesser extent, would justify their already preconceived notions. And therefore you got two camps dividing quite quickly: the revisionist camp, composed of people who thought that the Treaty of Versailles was unfair and should be revised, and the anti-revisionist camp, which essentially held Germany and Austria-Hungary primarily responsible."

By the 1930s the prevailing view was the one espoused by David Lloyd George, Prime Minister of Britain from

1916 to 1922. In 1918 Lloyd George had floated the idea that Kaiser Wilhelm II might be tried for war crimes. But in his 1934 memoir he wrote: "The nations slithered over the brink into the boiling cauldron of war ... not one of them wanted war; certainly not on this scale." As Ham says, the general feeling had become, "We're all to some extent to blame." This conciliatory view, which, as Mombauer notes, let Germany off the hook, remained largely unchallenged for two decades.

Two men, Italian Luigi Albertini and German Fritz Fischer, would change the direction of the debate once again. Langdon explains that Albertini was a political philosopher and a journalist who found himself unemployed under Mussolini's Fascist dictatorship because he would not toe the Fascist line. He became a researcher, and having known nearly all of the major participants in the July Crisis in 1914 because of his background as a political reporter, he interviewed them and consulted their diaries and their private papers. "The result is this enormous three-volume work that would have transformed the debate in 1942 had it been available in any language other than Italian," he says.

Albertini's work — which placed the primary blame for the war at Germany's feet — remained untranslated until 1957, when Isabella Massey brought it out in English as *The Origins of the War of 1914*. The effect, Langdon says, was explosive. "This was the Cold War and the Cold War rarely was much colder than it was in 1957. It was a very, very difficult period. Germany had become an ally of Great Britain and France and the United States in the North Atlantic Treaty Organization. West Germany was opposed to communism. East Germany, of course, was a satellite of the Soviet Union. So this argument over to what extent Germany was responsible for World War I resonated with people who held Germany entirely responsible for the outbreak of World War II."

The following year German historian Fritz Fischer read the translation. It was, says Langford, "a transformative moment for him". Fischer used German archive material, some of it previously unreleased, to test Albertini's conclusions, and published his work in two large volumes. In 1961 he released *Griff nach der Weltmacht* which, says Langdon, "is translated as *Germany's Aims in the First World War*, but really should be translated the way Fischer meant it, *The Grasp for World Power*, because he was very condemnatory of Germany's role in 1914".

Debates on German radio and German television in which Fischer would take on his critics had all of Germany mesmerised, says Langdon. They resonated throughout Europe, too, and Mombauer says this intense level of engagement makes sense when you consider the political climate of the time. "If you're looking at Europe, say from the vantage point of London, you can see the Soviet Union emerging as a potential threat, and Germany is much more important as a future ally than as a former enemy. So there is partly a sort of reassessing of what Germany means to the rest of Europe, the rest of the world."

Langdon says there is a post-Fischer consensus: "a general acceptance of primary culpability lying with Austria and Germany, but not absolving France, Russia and England of some measure of culpability." But views may well change again in the future. All four historians agree that our answers to the question of who started the Great War — "the evolution of blame", as Ham calls it — are always coloured by our own lives and times. "This is never just about the First World War," says Mombauer. "It's always about contemporary political concerns."

Margaret MacMillan gives an example of the way current issues and perceptions affect the discussion and how sensitive these issues are. "Serbians are very, very nervous now about the debate over the First World War because they think people will blame them for that and therefore look at Serbia today and say they're just the same ... What we historians can do is try to cut through some of that and keep reminding people that we're not blaming people today for anything. What we're trying to do is understand what happened."

2

LIONS AND DONKEYS

Were the generals truly incompetent?

Ludendorff: The English soldiers fight like lions.
Hoffmann: True. But don't we know that they are
lions led by donkeys.

— Alan Clark, *The Donkeys*, 1961

Just as our views of the causes of the Great War have changed over the years, so have our perceptions of its military leaders. Originally seen as brave and noble, they were later characterised by many as pompous fools. Nowhere is this more starkly evident than in the public image of Field Marshal Sir Douglas Haig, Commander-in-Chief of the British Expeditionary Force between 1915 and 1918.

For his leadership during the conflict and his staunch championing of returned servicemen afterward, Haig was a British hero. After his sudden death in 1928, more people lined the streets to pay their respects than would gather for Princess Diana seven decades later. But in the 1960s a combination of revisionist history and potent cultural influences led to a very different assessment of the war's military leadership as a whole and Haig as a case in point.

This view, which has persisted ever since, was summed up in a 2009 piece in *The Atlantic* magazine by Christopher Hitchens, who described the indelible imprint on the collective memory of "the teak-headed, red-faced, white-moustached general", ensuring his own safety and comfort in a chateau far from the fighting while he called on ridiculously outdated cavalry tactics to send the infantry to their deaths by the thousands. Haig, he wrote, was "the personification" of this kind of "bovine British militarist".

One of the key factors in this radical change was Alan Clark's 1961 book about the conflict, *The Donkeys*, which took its title from the exchange between two top-level German generals quoted at the beginning of this chapter. Clark attributed the recording of this exchange to the post-war memoir of German general Erich von Falkenhayn.

But Clark's biographer says Clark later admitted to having simply invented this attribution; he couldn't remember where he had come across the phrase.

In fact it first occurred in a different memoir, *An English Wife in Berlin*, by Evelyn, Princess Blücher, published in 1920, where it has a slightly different flavour. Blücher writes that she heard the following at German High Command, but does not attribute it to anyone in particular: "The English Generals are wanting in strategy. We should have no chance if they possessed as much science as their officers and men had of courage and bravery. They are lions led by donkeys." She goes on to write, "I wonder how much of this criticism is true."

However, Clark's version of the phrase and its origin stuck, and so did the perception it encapsulated: that of young lives wantonly wasted. Two years later the play *Oh What a Lovely War* opened in London based on this notion of brave, honest soldiers in the hands of uncaring, incompetent generals. In a piece spurred by its 2014 revival, *The Guardian*'s theatre critic Michael Billington describes the play's "devastating effect". Billington, who was in the audience of that first production, still had on hand the original program, which referred to the many "blunders" made during the conflict. The 1969 film version cemented this view in people's minds.

The other thing that happened around this time was a new interest in the work of British "war poets" such as Siegfried Sassoon and Wilfred Owen. Owen, in particular, "did not become important in people's understanding of war until the 1960s," says Professor Sir Hew Strachan, author of a number of books about the Great War and editor of *The Oxford Illustrated History of the First World War*. During the conflict and in the years that followed, "you didn't go to the poets in order to understand the war". But the views of Owen, with his anger at the waste of lives ("those who die as cattle"), and Sassoon with his mockery of the generals, struck a chord in the '60s, further strengthening the lions-and-donkeys perception. (For more on the literature of the war see Chapter 6.)

"There is no doubt that this has become the very dominant way of describing World War I, at least in the English-speaking world," says Professor Joan Beaumont, whose books include *Broken Nation: Australians and the Great War*. But why were we so willing to adopt this interpretation? "I think we have to acknowledge that in any situation of extreme trauma and crisis it's in the nature of human beings to find someone to blame," she says. "One of the things I think explains the ongoing fascination — and it's a very morbid fascination — with World War I is that the war itself seemed to acquire a momentum and a power which was beyond the capacity of any individual at any level to manage and control."

Professor Gary Sheffield, author of books including *The Somme: A New History* and *The Chief: Douglas Haig and the British Army*, rejects the idea that the upper ranks were more incompetent than not. He says that Clark, who went on to a long career as a Conservative politician in Britain, "was very open about his reason for writing *Donkeys*. He wanted to make money, and it made him a lot of money."

For Sheffield, "the phrase 'lions led by donkeys' is a travesty. Some generals were better than others. By the end of the war most of the bad ones had been pushed to one side and there was a meritocracy emerging. We are, of course, talking here specifically about the forces of Britain and the empire. I think you can make out quite a decent case that, for example, the Austro-Hungarian leadership were donkeys. But we fail to see British generalship in a wider context."

Professor Peter Stanley, whose 25 books include the co-authored *Australians at War, 1885–1972*, takes rather a different view, arguing that leadership did fail, at least in the early part of the war. He points out that Clark's book was subtitled *A History of the British Expeditionary Force in 1915*. "By the end of the war the British and everybody else had learned to do it better, but in 1915 nobody was doing it very well. You might feel pity for the generals being placed in a position where they were trying desperately to cope with a new form of warfare that nobody had experienced before. But, my goodness, did it take so many lives before they started to work out what should have been done better?"

The steep learning curve arose, says Joan Beaumont, because when the war began, it used a new style of warfare which demanded a very different style of leadership. Right up to the Second Boer War in 1899 generals had led their troops into battle. Given the scale of the battlefields in World War I and the use of trenches, that was no longer possible. As Beaumont puts it, "this kind of war requires a skill set which is very different from that of the past and leaves the generals open to criticism for not being classic heroes".

Hew Strachan explains that one of the reasons generals in the Great War were caricatured as staying cosily far from danger is that "trench warfare actually requires them to be in the rear. It creates a linear battlefield. You've got massive numbers of men, enormous logistic problems, real supply challenges, and so the general is less obviously a commander and more a manager of a sort of enormous enterprise, which requires being in an office at a desk."

Professor William Philpott, whose books include *Attrition: Fighting the First World War*, says the generals on the Western Front often *were* in chateaux, not because they were keeping out of harm's way, but simply because it was often the most practical solution. "You need a big building in which to put large numbers of signallers, staff officers, those other elements of the military establishment."

Even so, a remarkable number of generals were killed in action, many more than in World War II. In fact three British major-generals were killed in a single World War I battle, the Battle of Loos — as many as in the entire Second World War. Philpott notes that while the logistics of managing such a large operation required those sizable headquarters away from the frontlines, the available communications didn't allow the top brass to gather sufficient information during a fast-running battle, meaning they had to move to within sight of the fighting. And a general is just as vulnerable to shell-fire as a private.

Our historians, experts all, agree on these facts but they differ greatly in their assessments of decisions taken by the generals. And no figure is more divisive than Haig. Understanding their disagreement over specific decisions Haig made on the Western Front in France gives insight into why the lions-and-donkeys debate is still running hot.

Sheffield says that Haig "became highly effective but he, like everybody else, went through a learning process". The fiercest critics of his leadership reject this. As evidence of his incompetence they point to the way Haig, made British Commander-in-Chief six months earlier, conducted the Battle of the Somme in 1916.

For a week before the planned attack along a huge 24-km-long front, Allied artillery bombarded enemy lines. The intention was to smash the Germans' barbed-wire defences and concrete bunkers. Despite the deployment of an estimated 1.6 million shells, the major effect of this bombardment was to warn the German leaders of what was to come and give them time to prepare; their well-fortified lines suffered relatively little damage.

The whistles blew early on the morning of 1 July and 11 British divisions began walking towards the lines, believing their way to be clear. German troops were ready with machine guns. It turned into slaughter on an almost unimaginable scale. There were 60,000 British casualties, including 20,000 killed. Of all the British officers who went into battle that first day, 60 per cent died.

Modern-day critics condemn Haig for his entire approach to the battle, but particularly for going ahead with his plans despite supposedly being told that the German defences had not been destroyed. Gary Sheffield says this is not borne out by the facts. "Haig is definitely culpable for faulty artillery tactics at the beginning of the Somme. Basically, he spread his gunfire far too thinly. He allocated far too many targets to be attacked. But it seems very clear to me, having worked extensively in Haig's papers, that on the eve of battle he was unaware of the extent to which the wire had not been cut — in some places, not in all. The idea that Haig deliberately ignored uncomfortable evidence in this case is, I think, not true."

Sheffield also points out the realpolitik limitations on Haig. "People forget that Britain were the junior partners in a coalition (and in that sense the Australians were the junior partners to the junior partners). Haig did not want to fight on the Somme in July 1916. Given complete freedom of choice he would have fought up around Ypres and he would have fought at a later date when he had more troops, heavy guns, and maybe even tanks to hand. But that's what happens when you are the junior partner in a coalition. You do, on the whole, what the senior partner in the coalition wants to do. In that case, it's to fight in France at the behest of the French Commander-in-Chief."

It is, he continues, "very clear" that in the lead-up to the battle Haig told French Commander-in-Chief Marshal Joseph Joffre that he preferred not to fight there. "But like a good coalition partner, what he would do was make his point, sometimes quite forcefully, then if there was no alternative he would get on with it."

Joan Beaumont concurs. "I think we have to look at battles such as the Somme and the Third Ypres, which are the ones that Haig is generally castigated for, within the wider context of the war. Haig is fighting within an alliance which had its difficulties." It wasn't possible, she says, to abandon the Somme given that the French were fighting in Verdun and that one of the key political objectives of the Somme was to keep the French in the war.

"To me the big question when we criticise the way which the war was conducted is what alternatives both the commanders and the politicians may have had at the time. Once the Germans have occupied very valuable parts of France and Belgium, to have remained inactive was really to concede that to them." For Beaumont one of the persuasive arguments is that the British and the French commands "had to do something and, yes, the Somme may have been a pretty catastrophic something, but did you simply remain inactive until such time as technological change gave you some more advantages?"

From our modern perspective, the sheer scale of the casualties might seem shocking; an indictment of the leader's incompetence. But, says Professor Robin Prior, whose six books on the First World War include the co-authored *The Somme*, today we place a much higher value on each life, as evidenced by the attendance of prime ministers and heads of state in nations such as Australia at the funerals of individuals killed while serving their country. "Who could now contemplate 60,000 casualties on one day, as you had on the first day of the Somme?" he says.

The other great criticism of Haig is that he was simply unwilling to adapt to modern warfare and unable to concede when his tactics weren't working. Says Joan Beaumont, "He's often and justly criticised for continuing his great campaigns too long. What if the Third Ypres had finished in early October and he hadn't insisted on believing that the Germans were about to collapse and that he could take Passchendaele and that might bring about the end of the war? And what if the Somme had ended a little earlier? Would our judgment of him be more charitable?"

Gary Sheffield says that's all very well in theory, but the political pressures and ugly realities of war made those choices moot: "The Somme continued until the beginning of November basically because the French wanted to do so. Passchendaele is an even more heartbreaking story."

The Battle of Passchendaele, formally known as the Third Battle of Ypres, became a three-month-long nightmare that resulted in more than half a million casualties among the combatants. Haig had long wanted to fight in Flanders and the battle began with high hopes on the British side. Like the Somme it was preceded by a huge, sustained bombardment but, again like the Somme, this did not achieve its aim.

The battle itself began on 31 July 1917. The early days brought some successes for Haig's side, but then came the heaviest rain to have hit the area in three decades. The churned-up ground turned into mud so deep both men and horses drowned in it. But the Allies weren't the only ones to suffer and, says Sheffield, as October neared the Germans appear to be on the point of defeat and the weather improved. Haig then had to decide whether to cease battle or keep pushing on.

"He carries on and we know the result of that," says Sheffield, but, he adds, Haig's hands were, in essence, tied. "Effectively, you have three options. You either stay where you are on a terrible line which offers basically no defence; or you fall back to Ypres, thus abandoning everything that you've captured so far, which is psychologically and politically impossible; or you fight on up to the Passchendaele ridge to capture a line for future operations. It's an absolutely no-win situation and in the end I think Haig takes the only option that's realistically available to him."

Robin Prior and Peter Stanley disagree with Sheffield on this. They also disagree about Haig's battle tactics. Prior is particularly scathing of his use of cavalry. The continued attempts to use this "weapon from the 19th century" is, he says, "one of the great marks against Sir Douglas Haig …

He massed the cavalry before the Somme. He massed it before Passchendaele in 1917 and for God's sake he massed it on the 4th of November 1918! The cavalry had no role in the Western Front of any importance and yet Haig keeps on doing this."

Echoing Stanley's point about how long the lessons took, Prior says, "Although these people were learning, they were learning at a snail's pace, and what they were doing with their ludicrous plans that had no chance of success was casting away tens of thousands of people's lives. There is no way that you could fight the First World War cheaply, but you could fight it slightly less expensively than it was fought."

While willing to argue the case about Haig, whose work he examined at book length, Sheffield says, "we should be looking far more widely at the way the army developed and the way the command and control structure developed".

Indeed, Hew Strachan says there were structural problems in Allied leadership that far outweighed the deficiencies or otherwise of any individuals. The ability of generals to delegate effectively was, he says, the biggest deficiency in British High Command. "It's not necessarily the case in other armies, but if you think that the British Expeditionary Force is under 100,000 men when it goes to France in 1914 and that by the end of the war over five million would have served in the British Army, you realise that there's an enormous increase in expectation as to what these generals can do and how they can manage this war."

The biggest problem, he says, was that a whole layer of the hierarchy was missing: "Above all, there was a lack of qualified staff officers." Peter Stanley agrees wholeheartedly. "Generals decide things, but they get asked what to decide on by staff officers. So armies need staff officers to decide about everything from how much ammunition to how many casualties to how many men they should use … It was hard to find military men with those qualifications, and indeed with the attributes that enabled them to make calculations, make recommendations. The Germans were really good at it because they'd been doing it for about 75 years, but the British only discovered general staff officers in the late 19th century and so they didn't have very many."

Strachan says, "In abusing commanders and staffs we tend to forget that mass armies fighting industrialised war need these people as a critical skill more almost than they need any other critical skill. And it takes time to produce that critical skill. Four years was just about enough time for Britain to produce enough staff officers by 1918."

The German military organisation might have functioned well, but individual generals were another matter. Prior says, "I suppose what rather annoys me about 'lions led by donkeys' is it's always put in a British context. If you're looking for real donkeys in this war, try Ludendorff." Prussian general Erich Ludendorff (the one erroneously quoted by Alan Clark in his book) effectively ran Germany's war along with Chief of Staff Paul von Hindenberg. Ludendorff had early successes in the war but he followed these by pushing through disastrous policies such as the unrestricted submarine warfare that brought America into the conflict, and the huge, failed German offensive on the Western Front in 1918. Prior doesn't mince words in his assessment of the general who famously viewed peace as a mere interlude between wars, declaring him "a donkey *par excellence*".

There is also the example of Italian general Luigi Cadorna, who began executing men from the units of his own army that he decided hadn't fought fiercely enough, and who mounted machine guns behind his own lines to fire on anyone judged too tardy in going over the top. Peter Stanley says given half a chance Cadorna's troops would have turned their guns on him.

The modern-day assessment of Ludendorff and Cadorna is straightforward. But one military leader from the Central Powers, as Germany and its allies were known, evokes quite a different reaction: Mustafa Kemal Ataturk, whose success countering the Allied landing in the Dardanelles in 1915 set him on the path to becoming a Turkish national hero and, more surprisingly, a figure of respect for latter-day Australians. Peter Stanley says that Australians who condemn British generals as "hopeless" on Gallipoli because they sacrificed their men will simultaneously applaud Ataturk as a great genius and a wonderful military commander, "even though he sent his men against machine guns and ended up with thousands of them slaughtered".

The change in the Western perception of Ataturk and his soldiers over the years since the landing on Anzac Cove has been remarkable. Stanley says, "There's obviously more to this discussion than merely the debate of which tactics were effective at what time and who introduced them. There's an element of sentiment that comes into the discussion and national feeling, and for Australians that national feeling is different now to what it was during the war, and indeed for decades after."

Another change in Australia's national feeling has been the way we assess home-grown military leaders. Stanley notes that only relatively recently did Australians even begin to distinguish between Australian and British generals — prior to that they were a united force serving the cause of the empire, albeit with Australia in the junior role. Joan Beaumont says, "One reason the Australian commanders don't get quite such a bad press is because for much of the war they were at a relatively low level and therefore not making the major strategic decisions that the British and French commanders had to make. But it is striking how rarely Australian commanders really spoke up in protest against some of these more profligate operations. Occasionally they did, but generally like any military officer, they expressed such reservations as they felt able to express and then got on with the job."

General John Monash, who rose to become Commander of the Australian Corps in France, is widely seen as someone who was greatly concerned about casualties. Beaumont says this is because Monash had the great good fortune to come to command at a time when lot of harsh lessons had been learned, "and also, of course, the great technological changes that make victory possible have occurred". But if you look at how he handled, say, the attack on the Hindenburg Line, "some of the more rosy-eyed views of Monash might be qualified".

Stanley agrees and adds, "The problem with Australians is that they think that Monash is the only genius general in the Great War. But he's among a galaxy of British generals who come up through those terrible lessons in 1915, '16, '17 and finally in 1918, and finally work out how to do it." Monash, he says, wasn't the only general who learned quickly, he was the only *Australian* general who did.

In fact Monash's success centred on his suitability for the new type of war — had he fought in the 19th century it would have been a different story. Beaumont says his background as a civil engineer enabled him to understand logistics and calculate precisely, say, the number of shells needed for a particular section of the front. "All this data was something he was very skilled at being able to bring together. The skills you're looking for in Monash are not bravado and tactical heroism. Indeed, at Gallipoli, when

Monash did have to lead his troops up the steep slopes, he didn't perform particularly well."

Professor Margaret MacMillan, author of *The War that Ended Peace: The Road to 1914*, says that Monash and Canadian Arthur Currie exemplified the new mould of men who were promoted to the top during the war. They are the counter to what she calls the enduring myth "that all the generals were stupid and just sat behind the lines in French chateaux drinking champagne, when in fact, they were trying very, very hard to think of ways to break the deadlock".

Look beyond the broad brushstrokes of "lions" and "donkeys" and it becomes clear that (as with the war's causes) the truth is much more complex, and that our own contemporary events influence which parts of the story we choose to emphasise. Joan Beaumont says we often now see soldiers "as victims, not as heroes". This is very different to the way many of those who fought in World War I saw themselves: "Pompey Elliot, one of the more famous and charismatic commanders of Australians in World War I, boasted in 1918 about how efficiently Australians could kill Germans with a bayonet jab through the throat. If you go to a ceremony at the War Memorial today, you don't hear about people killing each other. You hear about people dying for their country."

A generation that responded to the Cold War threat of nuclear destruction by rejecting authority readily took up the "lions led by donkeys" idea. So much so that what began as a challenge to the orthodox view that World War I represented necessary sacrifice became itself the new orthodoxy. Now the "donkeys" view, in turn, is being questioned, reflecting the fact that, as Stanley says, "History is a relationship between society and its past." It is a debate that will continue long into the future.

3

"SIDE-SHOWS"

Was the fighting in the Pacific, the Middle East and the Alps a distraction?

The way to end this war is to kill Germans and not Turks. The place where we can kill most Germans is here and therefore every man and every round of ammunition we have got in the world ought to come here.

— British general Sir Henry Wilson on the Western Front, March 1915

For many in British High Command, the Western Front *was* the war, or it should have been. William "Wully" Robertson, who became Chief of the Imperial General Staff at the end of 1915, was one high-profile example. Robertson received his promotion shortly after submitting a memorandum to the War Cabinet that spoke of the dangers of Gallipoli and other "side-shows" that were drawing much-needed resources away from the fighting in France. This view was given strong public airing by Robertson supporter Charles à Court Repington, war correspondent for *The Times* for most of the conflict.

Others argued that facing the enemy in the Pacific, the Dardanelles and the Alps was strategically necessary and would divert Central Powers resources, giving the Allies a better chance in Western Europe. The soldiers on the ground had no say. Shipped to the beaches of Gallipoli or sent shivering into the mountains, they fought and died while the debates continued.

Australia suffered its first casualties of World War I less than a month into the war. The action was against German forces but it took place in the steamy tropics, 14,000 km from Europe.

In 1884 Germany had taken over the northeastern part of the huge island of New Guinea (whose western half was a Dutch colony) as well as nearby islands including New Britain, and even a port in China. Dr Christine Winter, Senior Research Fellow in History at the University of Sydney, says Australia was very unhappy about this.

In fact, Winter says, one of the first things Australia did as a federated nation was take possession of Papua, making the south-eastern section of Papua a British colony. It was keen to expand this holding, so when war was declared the nation was "ready and eager" to engage the Germans.

Germany's up-to-date navy patrolled the Pacific in the form of its East Asia Squadron, staying in touch via wireless- and telegraph-stations installed across the region. On 6 August 1914, two days after it had declared war on Germany, Britain asked Australia to raise a force to destroy these stations and seize German New Guinea.

The volunteer Australian Naval and Military Expeditionary Force (ANMEF), as it was named, consisted of 1,500 militia infantry and 500 naval reservists and ex-sailors. It was assembled remarkably quickly under the command of Boer War colonel William Holmes, and on 11 September reached a bay 80 km from the German colony's capital, Rabaul. A landing party of 25 Australians set off for the radio tower at Bita Paka, 30 km inland. German soldiers and New Guinean troops were waiting in ambush, but after several firefights, the ANMEF prevailed. Thirty New Guineans, six Australians and one German were killed in the surprisingly intense encounter.

Winter says it wasn't so much that "the Germans lost or the Australians won, but the New Guinean police soldiers (as the German literature calls them) decided not to fight anymore. They were the ones who actually decided the battle after 30 of them died, when they put down their weapons and surrendered." We know very little about these men, she says. This was partly because of colonial disregard, but also because the men's families were often "quite coy" about letting the Australians who came in to rule New Guinea know that their relatives had fought on the opposite side. It's an omission that historians are trying to redress, she says, noting that a higher per-capita percentage of Pacific Islanders than Australians fought in World War I.

After the Bita Paka action the ANMEF sailed around to Rabaul, where they were initially resisted by the German military and civilians and their governor, Eduard Haber. It was an uneven fight, Winter notes, with 1,500 Australians coming in to defeat 660 Germans, which included civilians like the post officer and the plantation owner. After a five-day siege of the inland town Toma, the Germans surrendered to Holmes. Under the terms of surrender, the German officials were repatriated but the civilians got to stay and continue with their lives. In fact, under League of Nations directions, the arrangement would outlast the war: "Australia, annoyed because they wanted to take over New Guinea, had to stick with that surrender agreement until 1921," says Winter.

But the loss of German territory in New Guinea did not eliminate the threat posed by the German Navy in the Pacific. "Germany had a trick up its sleeve: its ghost raiders," Winter explains. Warships in disguise, they were "going under a wrong flag, putting up fake chimneys to change their silhouette, and they were capturing ships".

The most famous of them was the *Wolf*. "It stayed hidden and in operation for 15 months," says Winter. "Never went ashore, but captured ships, raided the supplies, took the civilians and ship crew on board keeping them captive, and went on and captured the next ship. So people just disappeared in the region and Australia was getting very nervous and frightened: 'Where is *Wolf*?' 'Is she here?' 'Is she there?' 'Is *this* ship going to be taken?' 'Will my aunty safely arrive in America?'"

Serviced by its own spotter plane and fitted out with radio equipment powerful enough to stay in contact with Germany, the *Wolf* remained at large, destroying more than 30 enemy vessels and capturing more than 400 hostages: men, women and children, who were crammed aboard, "living with the crew, unable to leave, unable to contact anybody, half bored, half excited. It wasn't pretty," says Winter. Finally, after more than a year, the ship sailed back to Germany uncaught. Its story is one of the most extraordinary of the war — in a "side-show" or any other theatre.

Seven months after the ANMEF had reached New Guinea, the Gallipoli landings began in the narrow Turkish strait known now as the Dardanelles and in ancient times as the Hellespont. It was this lengthy and very costly campaign that would spur General Robertson to deliver the memo urging Britain's military leaders against pouring resources into other campaigns rather than putting everything they had into the Western Front.

The British had been eyeing the Dardanelles from as early as 1904; following a plea for assistance from their ally Russia at the beginning of 1915 they firmed up a plan to mount a seaborne assault, pushing through the strait in order to attack the Turkish capital, Constantinople (now Istanbul). Engaging the Turks would ease some of the pressure on Russia, which was fighting Ottoman forces in the Caucasus. It would also serve British strategic aims to keep shipping flowing through the Suez Canal, says Associate Professor Eugene Rogan, author of *The Fall of the Ottomans: The Great War in the Middle East* and *The Arabs: A History*.

The Suez provided a "vital link between the Dominions and the Western Front. As many of the Anzac forces, as well as Indian soldiers, made their way through the Red Sea towards the Mediterranean and France, they had to pass through Egypt and the Suez Canal. The Germans and their Ottoman allies targeted the canal as a first point of attack to try to stop the British war effort. So the British made it a high priority not just to defend the Suez Canal Zone but also to drive the Turks back."

The first step would be to secure the shores of the Dardanelles. But Harvey Broadbent, whose books include *Gallipoli: The Fatal Shore*, says that the British "seriously underestimated" their opponents based on what had happened in the years prior to the war.

In 1912, with Russia's encouragement, four countries that had often found themselves at odds — Montenegro, Serbia, Bulgaria and Greece — united as the Balkan League with the aim of wresting Macedonia from the

Ottoman Empire, along with as many other Ottoman holdings in Europe as possible. That October the League countries declared war on Turkey in what would be known as the First Balkan War.

To the Ottomans' shock they were quickly and comprehensively defeated. In fact their troops were forced all the way back to the outskirts of Constantinople. By 3 December an armistice had been agreed upon, but an internal coup by the groups known as the "Young Turks" saw the Ottomans re-enter the fray, only to be defeated again, this time definitively. In the peace treaty it signed in May 1913, the empire lost all of its European territory.

A month after the treaty was signed, Bulgaria, feeling cheated out of its share of the spoils of war, turned on its former allies and began the Second Balkan War. This time Turkey joined with Serbia, Greece and Romania to quash Bulgaria, which lost much of what it had gained in the first war.

Broadbent says that the British regarded Turkey as "a bit of a pushover because of its lack of success earlier". They also thought the Ottomans were overstretched, fighting as they were on three fronts already: "They had the Middle East in Palestine–Sinai. They had the Persian Gulf. They had the Caucasus against the Russians ... this may be one of the things which encouraged the British and French to launch the attack at Gallipoli."

But there was a crucial difference in the Dardanelles. Here the Turks "were defending their homeland and this gave them an extra motivation". As well, "the Turkish commanders were experienced. They'd been hardened by the previous war experiences. Their first units were well trained and they had lot of motivation amongst the ordinary soldiers as well as the officers."

The Turks had excellent intelligence too. Some came via their foreign embassies, but they also made use of a brand-new technology: airplanes. "They used aircraft consistently — German aircraft in the main, using Turkish observers," says Broadbent. Daily flights allowed them to be very aware of what their enemy was doing. "They knew everything about the Allied forces gathering for the invasion on Lemnos and Imbros islands. Then during the campaign they knew about troop movements and ship movements."

There was even an attempt at an airborne assassination which originated with Turkish Deputy Commander-in-Chief Enver Pasha, who had led the Young Turks to power. Broadbent says that while his generals were focused on containing the Allies, Enver wanted more: "He was always pushing for ideas." He decided to "decapitate" the British force by eliminating the commander of the Allied operation, Sir Ian Hamilton. Enver sent his commanders a map showing the location of Hamilton's flagship with instructions to dispatch an armed plane. It almost worked. "The plane came over and it dropped its two or three bombs, but they missed," says Broadbent.

The Hamilton plan might have failed but the Turks did succeed in holding back the British, Australian, New Zealand, French and Indian troops — almost half a million in total — who poured onto their beaches. For nine months the campaign dragged on in deadly stalemate, the opposing lice-ridden trenches so close each side could hear the others speaking. By the time the last men were evacuated in January 1916 the Allies had suffered 250,000 casualties, including 46,000 deaths. The Turks had a similar number of overall casualties but around 20,000 more deaths.

As to whether Gallipoli was a "side-show", Broadbent says it did have a significant effect in that "it kept the whole Turkish army, the Fifth Army, away from the other theatres of war". On the other hand, "what would have happened to all those British and Anzac troops if Gallipoli hadn't happened? They would have been fighting in France, which would probably have added a lot more weight to the Western Front and may have made a difference there."

While the casualties suffered at Gallipoli made it a costly campaign for Turkey, Broadbent says that knowing it had resisted the might of the British Empire was a big boost for the morale of its people. However, while Turkey ran the Ottoman Empire, the Turks formed only part of its overall population. The remaining part of the empire stretched all the way down the Arabian Peninsula to what is now Yemen and Oman. Of the 22 million people under Ottoman rule when the war began, ethnic Turks made up only around 12 million. The rest consisted of various peoples, including many Arabs.

Salim Tamari, Director of the Institute of Palestine Studies and Adjunct Professor at the Center for Contemporary Arab Studies at Georgetown University, says that in earlier times the Turks had taken a reasonably decentralised approach, giving "a substantial amount of autonomy to the Syrian provinces and the other outlying provinces in the Ottoman Empire". For a long time things ran fairly smoothly, but "at the end of the 19th century nationalism became a force and started a wave of inter-ethnic conflict in which many of these areas became aware of their own difference from Istanbul".

Eugene Rogan says, "If you look at the six years before the outbreak of the First World War the Ottoman Empire had really been on something of a rollercoaster ride. The Young Turks overthrew the very autocratic government of Sultan Abdul Hamid II in a constitutional revolution in 1908, which raised hopes across the empire among Arabs, Armenians, Kurds and Turks that it would be the dawn of a new age of progress and reform, better able to adapt to the demands of the time."

These hopes were dashed. The instability that followed the revolution dragged the Ottomans into "a series of devastating wars — in 1911 with Italy over Libya and then the two Balkan Wars — which meant that instead of being strengthened by their constitutional revolution, the Ottoman Empire and the Young Turk rulers were really quite exhausted by 1914. Morale on both the Turkish and the Arab sides of the empire was quite low." Then came the war itself, which proved to be a time of "scarcity, of want, of hunger and of fear", Rogan says, and brought great suffering to many of the empire's subjects.

Conscription began, and for the first time also applied to the non-Muslim minorities, Jews and Christians. They fought on a wide variety of fronts: the Caucasus, Gallipoli, Mesopotamia (now Iraq) and the Suez front near Beersheba. "The Ottoman administration used to send soldiers as far away from the home front as possible to pre-empt possibilities of desertion," says Tamari.

In November 1914, Hamid's successor, Sultan Mehmed V, had called for Muslims all over the world to join the Ottoman struggle (for more on this see Chapter 7). The British were already very concerned that this call to arms would be heeded in various parts of their empire, notably India. Two serious setbacks close together — the withdrawal from Gallipoli and then a defeat in the battle of Kut al-'Amarah in Mesopotamia — made the British determined to find a way to weaken their opponent.

What happened at Kut deeply shocked Britain. After a series of easy victories which had secured the crucial Anglo-Persian oil pipeline in the southwest of Mesopotamia, the War Office instructed the 6th (Poona) Division of its British Indian Army to push on and capture

Baghdad. The troops made it to Ctesiphon, almost within reach of their goal, but here Turks engaged them in fierce battle. Soundly defeated, the Poona Division fell back in a harrowing 12-day retreat to the garrison town of Kut al-'Amarah, where, on 7 December, the pursuing Turks besieged them.

The besieged troops expected a relief force to appear within days. But three relief attempts were stopped by the Turks at a cost of 23,000 British casualties and the trapped soldiers endured a hellish 147 days of near-starvation, disease, freezing temperatures, floods and bombardment before surrendering. The treatment meted out to the survivors saw more than a third die either on the march to prisoner-of-war camps in Anatolia or once they had arrived.

Coming on top of the Ottoman victory in Gallipoli, Kut was a humiliating blow to the British. They became increasingly convinced of the need to weaken their opponents by trying to foment revolt from within. Could they persuade the Arabs to turn against their rulers?

Even before the war Britain had been working to build strategic Arabic alliances, but fear of reprisal deterred many Arabs from showing disloyalty to the Ottomans, at least openly. Nationalism was "the great red line" for the Ottomans, says Rogan. "Nationalism had been the means of the break-up of Ottoman territory right across the Balkans as Bulgaria, Serbia, Montenegro emerge from being provinces of the Ottoman Empire into independent states. And the Ottomans were determined not to see the Arabs go the same way."

This meant, he says, that before 1914 "the scope to talk nationalist politics was very limited and those who did so engaged in secret societies whose views were really about trying to gain more autonomy for the Arab provinces under the Ottoman Empire as a kind of Turko-Arab empire, maybe on the model of the Austro-Hungarian. The one thing Arab nationalists before the First World War were concerned about was that if they left the Ottoman Empire they'd be vulnerable to European domination; as events were to prove, they were quite right."

But in 1916, having suffered major defeats at Ottoman hands, the British were determined to incite Arab unrest. Their goal, Rogan says, was to build an alliance with a credible Islamic authority to open an internal front against the Ottoman Empire. They found an ideal partner in the Sharif of Mecca, Hussein bin Ali, leader of the

Hashemite clan. Under the wartime alliance with the British, Sharifian forces received financial support, arms and materiel to launch a revolt, and Hussein received the promise of post-war Arab independence.

In June 1916 Hussein declared that his people were in revolt. The British hoped this uprising would spread throughout the region, becoming a great Arab revolt that would overthrow Ottoman rule. In an attempt to move things along, young British intelligence officer T.E. Lawrence joined Hussein's son Prince Feisal, taking arms and gold to help him "bring the Arab Revolt to full glory". In his post-war memoir *Seven Pillars of Wisdom*, Lawrence recalled, "In my view, if the revolt did not reach the main battlefield against Turkey it would have to confess failure, and remain a side-show of a side-show."

But the Turks weren't going to cede control easily. "The repression the Ottomans meted out to anyone who took a disloyal line towards the Ottoman government was extremely harsh: exile, executions," says Rogan. "So for the most part, people in the Arab provinces of the Ottoman Empire were fence-sitters ... they were fearful of what the Ottomans would do to them and they took a wait-and-see approach to the Arab Revolt, which never really did engender the broad-based mass support that either the Hashemites or the British had hoped it might."

One of the figures who inspired much fear was Turkish general Djemal Pasha, one of the "Three Pashas" who ruled the empire. He was nicknamed *al-Saffah*, meaning "the Blood Shedder", says Rogan. But while Djemal was "much despised" by Arab nationalists when they had the freedom to speak up after the war, "what's striking if you read contemporary accounts is how people in the Arab provinces really deferred to Djemal Pasha and courted his favour. The response in the general public to executions of Arab nationalists in Damascus, in Beirut in 1916, was remarkably muted."

In *Year of the Locust: A Soldier's Diary and the Erasure of Palestine's Ottoman Past*, Salim Tamari gives us a window into the life of Arabs within the empire. In the book Tamari translates and puts into historical context the wartime diaries of Ihsan Hasan Turjman, a clerk and foot soldier from a learned family in Jerusalem, in what was then Palestine. Turjman was conscripted in November 1914 and killed in 1917, having served mostly at the southern front near Beersheba and as a clerk in the Jerusalem garrison.

Tamari says Turjman saw himself very much as a part of the empire. "As the war progressed he became increasingly hostile to both the army and the state, but he always thought of himself as an Ottoman citizen and he identified as an Arab within the Ottoman regime." He was, however, initially very open to the idea of the Arab Revolt. "He saw the revolt as a bright spot in a dismal war that was going nowhere and he greeted it enthusiastically," says Tamari.

The higher-ups weren't so sure. "The intelligentsia and the officer corps in the Arab armies of the Ottoman Empire were divided on the issue and there were a substantial number of soldiers and officers who continued to fight for the Ottomans, who continued to support the Ottoman war, even at the height of the rebellion," Tamari says. "It's very hard to find statistics but I would say from circumstantial evidence that many more soldiers and officers continued to voluntarily fight with the Ottomans" than otherwise. However, he adds, most of the Arab population was not politically engaged on either side; they just wanted relief from the devastation, havoc, disease and death that the war had brought.

Turjman didn't live to see Jerusalem fall to the British in December 1917 but he witnessed its citizens' suffering, which had begun in 1915, because, says Tamari, of natural disasters including a locust attack and food shortages produced by the naval blockade established by the French and British. The result was famine. The fact that the young men were off fighting compounded the problems for their families, resulting in "the collapse of the social order. Jerusalem was not the only town hit. Beirut, Damascus, Jaffa, all the coastal cities were badly hit by the war".

Tamari says contemporary Arabs view those years in the light of two major events. One was the agreement reached secretly in 1916 between the British and French governments with input from Russia, known as the Sykes–Picot Agreement. This "divided Greater Syria and Iraq into Balkanised states in which sectarianism, religion and regional interest played to the inter-imperial rivalry between France, Britain, Italy and — of course, before the Bolshevik revolution — the Russian state". The other was 1917's Balfour Declaration in support of creating a Jewish national home in Palestine, which, he says, removed the possibility of including Palestine in a mooted independent Arab state to be created after the war under Sharif Faisal. These events and the changes they wrought "became part of the patrimony of the war in people's minds today".

World War I accounted for only a tiny part of the Ottoman Empire's long existence but Tamari and Rogan agree that those years irrevocably shaped how Arabs assess their entire four centuries as citizens of the empire. Rogan says, "Most people view the Ottomans through the prism of the misery of the First World War, and it really fed an Arab nationalist line in the 1920s and '30s that blamed the Ottomans for holding the Arab world back. The war years were just unbelievably horrible for people living in the Arab world. It's no surprise that since that's their last experience of Ottoman rule it tainted their entire experience of Ottoman rule in hindsight."

Thousands of miles away another "side-show" was underway in the mountains along the border between Austria-Hungary and Italy. It too engendered great misery, albeit of a completely different kind.

Despite being part of the pre-war Triple Alliance with Germany and Austria-Hungary, Italy remained neutral for the first 10 months of hostilities. Then in May 1915 it declared war on Austria-Hungary. This made a new front of the entire 600-km-long border between the two countries, a development that was welcomed by the existing Entente Allies because it drew Austro-Hungarian troops from the Eastern Front, thereby bringing some relief to Russia.

The Italian army was dreadfully under-equipped in general, but the underfed, poorly clad soldiers who fought in the mountains had a particularly horrendous time of it. Never before had war been conducted in terrain like the narrow mountain peaks and glaciers of the Dolomites and the Julian Alps, with fighting taking place at altitudes as high as 3,000 metres. Artillery had to be dragged up vertical cliff faces in temperatures far below freezing point. A million men died, three-quarters of them on the Italian side. At least as many froze to death or were killed by avalanches as were killed by the enemy. Italian poet Giuseppe Ungaretti, who served in the mountains, said that for him snow was "truly a sign of mourning". The colour white, he wrote, "gives me the sense of things ending".

Ernest Hemingway saw the conflict first-hand, having volunteered as an ambulance driver for the American Red Cross in Italy. The writer, who fictionalised his experiences in 1929's *A Farewell to Arms*, described the Italian Front as "the most colossal, murderous, mismanaged butchery" of whole war.

As if the waste of life wasn't already great enough, the Italian units were terrorised by their murderous supreme commander General Luigi Cadorna, whom we met briefly in Chapter 2. *A Farewell to Arms* includes a faithful depiction of one of the executions of their own, designed to terrify the soldiers into fighting with sufficient vigour, in which Cadorna specialised.

Cadorna was finally removed in 1917 after a successful Austro-Hungarian counter-attack at Caporetto, which pushed the Italian army so far back that the Austrians seized land that was home to 1.5 million Italians, thousands of whom then starved to death.

Following this disaster British and French troops were diverted to the Italian Front, losing the tactical advantage its existence had given the Entente Allies previously. Under the steady hand of Cadorna's replacement, General Armando Diaz, Italy was able to hold out long enough to finally seize victory in 1918 as the Central Powers collapsed. But in a familiar story, Italians felt they did not receive their dues in the post-war carve-up of Europe, and Fascist Benito Mussolini fuelled the resentment in order to seize power and set about taking what was supposedly owed.

It's clear that although the Pacific, the Middle East and the Italian Alps were far from the suffocating mud of Flanders, as were other oft-overlooked theatres of the war, Greece and east and southwest Africa, they are just as worthy of our attention. "Side-shows" doesn't begin to do them justice.

4

THE ENEMY WITHIN

Were those who objected traitors to the cause?

*We have lost our honor, our citizenship and all rights
to which a citizen is entitled ...*

— Imprisoned US Conscientious Objector Jesse Brenneman's
testimony to the Mennonite Church's Peace Problems Committee

The outbreak of war was not greeted with patriotic fervour by everyone. Those who objected to it, who refused to accept their leaders' claims that it was necessary, might have been in the minority, but they upheld their beliefs staunchly and often at great personal cost.

One of the most high-profile campaigners against the war was Bertrand Russell, the mathematician and philosopher whose father had twice served as British prime minister. In August 1914, just after hostilities had commenced, Russell laid his feelings bare in a letter to *The Nation* magazine: "All this madness, all this rage, all this flaming death of our civilisation and our hopes has been brought about because of a set of official gentlemen, living luxurious lives, mostly stupid, and all without imagination or heart, have chosen that it should occur, rather than that any one of them should suffer some infinitesimal rebuff to his country's pride."

Pacificists and anti-war campaigners had a range of motivations but generally they fell into two camps: socialists, and those who objected to fighting on religious grounds. Associate Professor Bobbie Oliver, author of *Peacemongers: Conscientious Objectors to Military Service in Australia, 1911–1945*, says that among the latter were Christadelphians, Jehovah's Witnesses and Quakers (or Society of Friends members) as well as Seventh Day Adventists, "who didn't actually object to military service, but ... were very much against doing any work on the Sabbath", including military duties.

Enlisting was voluntary in the early part of the war but those who didn't volunteer, on principle or otherwise, were often judged harshly. Oliver says that young men who were still serving in shops once the war had started were sometimes rounded on in public, particularly by women.

Women were also the main senders of white feathers as a mark of perceived cowardice. Oliver describes a case in Queensland where the anonymous sender "actually went to the trouble of punching a hole in the envelope so the end of the feather stuck out, and the feather was sent to the young man's work address". In fact the recipient had tried to enlist and been turned down.

In the face of that kind of hostility, anyone publicly objecting to the war had to be fired up by strongly held beliefs. For many those were left-wing political beliefs, specifically socialism. "Mostly, the opposition to the war came from Marxists," says Robert Bollard, author of *In the Shadow of Gallipoli: The Hidden History of Australia in World War I*. "They opposed it on the basis that it was a war between empires; it wasn't in the interest of working people." As a socialist slogan of the day put it, "A bayonet is a weapon with a worker at both ends."

One of the most vociferous socialist anti-war campaigners in Australia was Tom Barker. Born in England, Barker had enlisted in the British Army as a teenager just after the turn of the century and served three years before being discharged as medically unfit. He emigrated to New Zealand, where he was active in the Socialist Party and became an organiser for the Industrial Workers of the World (IWW — often called simply 'the Wobblies'). In 1914 Barker moved to Australia, where he relentlessly criticised the federal Labor government and its involvement in the war, a stance that saw him and his fellow agitators labelled traitors.

Their activities and those of others with an anti-war stance were tolerated, just, in the early part of the war, when voluntary enlistment was still running strong. The numbers signing up peaked just after Australian and New Zealand troops reached Gallipoli in April 1915, inspired by what Bollard calls "a completely over-the-top and somewhat fanciful account of the landing" from British journalist Ellis Ashmead-Bartlett, who wrote glowingly of strapping, fearless, "almost superhuman" soldiers. But propaganda wasn't the only reason why young men signed up. "Australia was in recession at the beginning of the war, and the peak of unemployment was at that same point," Bollard says. "It's still hard to know exactly how much enthusiasm for the landing at Gallipoli and how much the fact that unemployment was at 11 per cent encouraged that rush of recruitment."

Certainly as the truth about what was happening in the Dardanelles began to filter back, enthusiasm to join the fight waned. "They couldn't hide the fact that month after month no progress was made on Gallipoli," says Bollard. "And they also couldn't hide the fact that casualties were happening at an extraordinary rate, as these casualty lists were printed in the newspaper. The August battles were particularly bloody — Lone Pine and The Nek — and you can see at that point that recruitment begins to dwindle. Unemployment was lessening so we still don't know exactly how much that's got to do with it. But a little bit later on, in 1916 when the Australians were introduced to the Western Front and had as many casualties in a few days' fighting in Fromelles and Pozières as the whole nine months of the Gallipoli campaign, there was a devastating drop in recruitment."

In October 1915 Billy Hughes had taken over the prime ministership of Australia when Andrew Fisher stepped down. He had no tolerance for dissent and in a January 1916 speech urged more men to enlist, saying, "I appeal to the manhood of Australia. I do not appeal to those men who, posing as lovers of liberty, do what they can to prevent men joining the Expeditionary Forces." Those men, Hughes went on, "are foul parasites ... In the name of unionism and laborism, I pass them out like devils out of swine."

Soon after, Hughes travelled to England and then on to France, where he visited Australian troops on the Western Front. He was, says Bobbie Oliver, "very taken by the effort of the soldiers, but also he was pressured by the High Command in Britain to get more men". The British wanted 16,500 more men right away, then thousands more each month. In 1915 Hughes had declared, "In no circumstances would I agree to send men out of this country to fight against their will." But now, says Oliver, he decided "the only way that you could get the kind of numbers they thought they required was conscription". On his arrival back in Australia at the end of July, Hughes set about introducing it. Men were already required to train for home service when called up but he wanted to extend this to compulsory fighting overseas.

There were certainly supporters of the idea. But Hughes had seriously underestimated the depth of opposition both in his Labor Party and in Australia as a whole. The result was what Bollard describes as "an incredible polarisation", which Hughes failed to see. Stymied by the Senate's refusal to pass conscription legislation, he decided to take the issue to the people, convinced they would back him.

"Billy Hughes assumed he was going to win easily," says Bollard. "He had the press completely on side; he had powers of censorship; a War Precautions Act, where he jailed people regularly for actions prejudicial to recruiting; he banned lots of anti-conscription publications from circulation through the mail. And, if that wasn't sufficient, you also had soldiers, new recruits, being encouraged to leave their camp and basically destroy anti-conscription meetings. The first two attempts to hold anti-conscription rallies in the Domain in Sydney, for instance, were broken up by soldiers; in the second one police recorded that the people there were lucky to escape with their lives."

The Wobblies were among those targeted, for their distribution of anti-conscription pamphlets. Barker was arrested and spent a week in jail after refusing to pay a fine. Subsequently nine IWW agitators were prosecuted under the Unlawful Assemblies Act. Barker was among them; convicted of making statements prejudicial to recruiting, he was sentenced to six months' prison with hard labour. Before long the IWW itself was outlawed.

The referendum was set for the end of October. Hughes was so sure of the result, says Bollard, "they actually began calling people up, conscripting people a month before the referendum". These men found themselves at the Billy Hughes Training Camp at Goulburn Showground, where they were nicknamed "the Hughesiliers".

Opposition, however, continued to grow. Bollard says, "The third attempt to hold a rally in the Domain in Sydney was successful because 80,000 trade unionists — what the *Sydney Morning Herald* described as the bone and sinew of the labour movement — turned up to defend the meeting against the soldiers. The soldiers arrived, took one look at the crowd and gave up pretty quickly. And that was the turning point, in Sydney especially."

Despite bitter campaigning in which the accusations flung against those who opposed conscription included that they were in league with Germany or supported Ireland's anti-British Sinn Féin, the referendum was defeated. It was a close-run thing, though. "Australia was split right down the middle," says Bobbie Oliver. "Although most people would have regarded themselves as pro-war and very much strongly in support of the empire, they still objected to the principle of people being forced to go to serve." The Hughesiliers were quietly disbanded.

Conscription wasn't the only thing dividing the nation and leading to claims of disloyalty. Bollard says, "One of the most forgotten impacts of the war is that it didn't just kill people, it made people hungry." In 1920 the Royal Commission into the Basic Wage reported that, in real terms, wages between 1914 and 1919 fell by around 30 per cent. "Imagine a 30 per cent drop in the purchasing power of your wage," he says. "It's dramatic, especially in a time when people had much less fat, so as to speak, to shed."

Workers responded with strikes. It began, says Bollard, in Broken Hill, which had "probably the most radical group of workers in Australia ... They went on strike in January 1916 for a 44-hour week and a wage rise and they succeeded, mainly because they were supplying most of the lead for the Western Front, so they were in a very strong position. They were denounced as traitors but they won, and this opened the floodgates. There was a strike wave which rolled through the rest of 1916, culminating in a coal strike which happened pretty much as the first referendum was happening. The miners went on strike, and won a wage rise and a 40-hour week."

Further strikes followed in 1917 and that year conscription reared its head again. Hughes had been expelled from the Labor Party for his pro-conscription stance following the 1916 referendum. Having formed a new party — the Nationalists — he won the May 1917 federal election easily. While campaigning, he had promised not to revisit the issue of conscription unless "the tide of battle which flows strongly for the Allies turns against them". Just six months later he declared that this had happened and, "in view of the increasing gravity of the military situation", set a second referendum for late December 1917.

It too was defeated, this time by a larger margin. The result, says Oliver, was partly testament to Australia's war-weariness more than three years into the conflict and partly to the strong anti-conscription campaign featuring influential figures such as Archbishop Daniel Mannix, the head of the Catholic Church in Melbourne and a fierce opponent of Hughes's plan. This rejection of conscription was very unusual in international terms. In fact of all the combatant nations in World War I, only Australia and South Africa did not introduce it.

For the early part of the war, the experience of New Zealand mirrored that of its large neighbour and fellow member of the empire. As in Australia there were those who opposed the idea of going to war, but they were very much in the minority. David Grant, author of *Field Punishment No 1: Archibald Baxter, Mark Briggs and New Zealand's Anti-Militarist Tradition*, says the few objectors, principally Christian pacifists, "were very much swimming against the tide. The feeling was that we needed to go and support the mother country in times of stress. Initially people rushed to enlist. In the period from the outbreak of war up to the landing at Gallipoli, there were plenty of men to fulfil the requirements."

But in New Zealand, too, things changed as the ugly truth about Gallipoli began to filter back. "Cynicism slowly began to intrude and the numbers of men enlisting slowly decreased," Grant says. Conscription was seen as the answer and New Zealand's parliament passed it into law in August 1916 without need for referendum.

Which is not to say there was universal public approval. In fact, says Grant, "there was quite vigorous opposition. Mostly from left-wing Labour people, who believed if you're going to have conscription of men you must have conscription of wealth. But there were also significant numbers of others: Irish people living in New Zealand who felt it wasn't their fight; there were some Maori people who believed it wasn't their fight either; and there were a number of fundamentalist Christian people who felt that it wasn't their war, there shouldn't be war, and they weren't going to fight. But the great bulk of them were people of extreme left-wing persuasion."

The men of service age who continued to oppose taking part in the war even after conscription had been introduced were vilified as "shirkers" or "bludgers". Only those given official Conscientious Objector (CO) status were exempt and the only people automatically listed as COs were Quakers and Christadelphians — although, Grant notes, a number of Quakers did serve in non-combatant roles as stretcher-bearers.

Others who objected to serving had to apply for CO status. Hundreds registered, says Grant, and then had to justify their position to an appeal board. "The men appointed to these appeal boards had an inbuilt bias against men who did not want to fight; they felt it was a failure of citizenship on their part, and they were most unsympathetic. If your appeal was denied, and that was most likely, you had to choose whether you would swallow your scruples and enlist. If so, you had the option to enlist as a non-combatant — a medical orderly or clerk, or a stretcher-bearer as many of them did, though of course stretcher-bearers were out on the front and in danger of being wounded and killed just like soldiers were." Those who continued to refuse were imprisoned and, on release, set to work under close probation, often in forestry. "Some of these men were called up again and if they refused a second time would serve another term of imprisonment."

But imprisonment paled next to the shocking treatment handed out to 14 of New Zealand's objectors. Grant says that the then minister of defence, James Allen, believed that men who had failed their appeal boards were still part of the army. They were locked up in military camps and the overflow sent to civilian prisons. Then suddenly one morning in 1917 Colonel Herbert Potter, Commandant of the Trentham Military Camp near Wellington, decided to divest his camp and also some of the prisons. In particular he targeted the imprisoned objectors. "There was a troop ship in Wellington, the *Waitemata*, which had some space, so Potter decided that these men would be woken up, frogmarched down to the ship and taken to Britain and then France," Grant says. The thinking was "that when these 14 men saw the others fighting valiantly against the Germans in terrible conditions on the Western Front they would automatically change their minds and serve alongside their fellows".

In due course most of the men submitted and served as stretcher-bearers. But two, Archibald Baxter and Mark Briggs, never gave in, despite suffering what can only be described as torture in a military camp in France. "Both men were strung up on poles. This was called 'Field Punishment Number One'." Having survived this but still refusing to serve, Baxter was told to march to another part of the Western Front. "Weak, dazed and starving, he lost his way and ended up semi-conscious in a field, having divested himself of the uniform that they had made him wear. He was found semi-conscious and close to death by some British soldiers and gradually nursed back to health."

Baxter was later sent to a hospital that housed soldiers suffering shell shock and here he was diagnosed as insane. This was, says Grant, "an out for the New Zealand Army, because I think that the hierarchy had realised that he was never going to submit."

The treatment inflicted on Briggs included being beaten and dragged along duckboard by four soldiers on the orders of a military police sergeant who was determined to break him. "Duckboard" was the rough planks that formed walkways through the mud leading to the frontline — Briggs was pulled by his legs, and bled heavily from deep lacerations to his back. "He was in deep pain but refused to cry out," says Grant, who describes Briggs's spirit as unquenchable. "He simply did not protest and he did not submit." Finally, under instructions from army hierarchy, a medical board made the ruling that "he had rheumatism and therefore he was re-graded as C-2, unfit for combat action".

Conscription was just as contentious in "the mother country" itself, as Cyril Pearce, author of *Comrades in Conscience: The Story of an English Community's Opposition to the Great War*, explains. "It could be said to have divided the Liberal Party, who were in government at the time, because the Liberal Party had this long-standing commitment to individual conscience, the freedom of the individual to act according to his own view." Nonetheless conscription was introduced in Britain in January 1916 for single men and four months later for married men.

It's impossible to be certain how many men sought Conscientious Objector status, because in the 1920s the British government ordered relevant records to be destroyed. Pearce's research suggests there were at least 20,000 men throughout England, Scotland and Wales who appeared before tribunals explaining their refusal to serve.

Their experience varied greatly depending where they came from. "In some areas, such as parts of Lancashire, the tribunal system was not exactly sympathetic to war resistors but at least prepared to give them the benefit of the doubt. In many cases, because these areas were important parts of the war machine in terms of manufacturing cloth, engineering and so on, they were prepared to accept that these men had war-essential occupations, set aside their conscientious objection and say, 'You are exempt because you are in important occupation.' Whereas in other parts of the country, you'd find tribunals taking a very, very aggressive stance."

Those who were granted an exemption often had to serve anyway, says Pearce. "A non-combatant corps was created in the spring of 1916 and the government naively thought that it was the place where most conscientious objectors would prefer to serve. Some 3,000 of them did.

About 600 were sent over to France, and they served over there in behind-the-lines occupations, quarrying road stone to repair the roads going up to the front, in depots loading and unloading trains, and so on."

But "in the region of 1,500 men refused to have anything to do with military service. They were drafted, but refused to sign their army papers, refused to have medicals, refused to put on the uniform, and so on. And in various places they were subject to physical bullying and mistreatment. Something like 70 COs died either in prison or as result of the treatment they received in the army barracks," says Pearce.

Others were repeatedly imprisoned in an attempt to break their resolve. "They were initially court-martialled and sent down to prison with hard labour for about three months. Then they would come out, go back to their army unit, refuse to obey orders again and be court-martialled and sent to prison again. By the end of the war, they were being sent down for two-year stretches at a time. Many of them were court-martialled three and four times and there were some who were court-martialled as many as five or six times. They were even being court-martialled in the spring of 1919."

It is perhaps surprising that those in the USA — home of free will — who objected to fighting on religious or ideological grounds were also subject to mistreatment and vilification. But they were indeed, explains Professor Scott Bennett, author of *Radical Pacifism: The War Resisters League and Gandhian Nonviolence in America, 1915–1963*.

America entered the war in April 1917, two months after Germany had begun unrestricted submarine warfare against any ship, including officially neutral US vessels, in war-zone waters. (A policy of attacking commercial shipping early in the war had, in effect, been suspended in late 1915. See Chapter 10 for more.) The American government's decision had widespread, if not universal, domestic support. But conscription was another matter. It was seen by many "as something that violated the notion of liberty. So the opposition was widespread," says Bennett. As well, "many ethnic Americans, particularly German Americans, not only opposed intervention, they also opposed conscription because they did not want to end up in a situation where they were fighting against family and kin." Then there were Irish Americans "who detested the British — this was not long after the Easter Rebellion — and they certainly did not want to fight on behalf of the British".

A large number of Americans tried to evade conscription. Many simply failed to enrol as required in June 1917. Thousands of others, says Bennett, found themselves a wife "under the mistaken notion that if they were married, they would not be conscripted".

Others sought formal recognition as Conscientious Objectors. "There were some 20,000 objectors who were actually inducted into the army. And some 16,000 of them dropped their objections once they were in, often because they were pressured or brutalised by the army officers and the other men in the camps. But, ultimately, there were 4,000 who stuck to their positions. Approximately 1,300 of them did non-combatant medical service in the army, which is analogous to what happened in Britain. Another 1,300 did farm work."

Bennett estimates that there were some 450 "absolutist COs", who refused any and all cooperation with the military. "They were court-martialled, they were sentenced to life imprisonment or 25 years, and the conditions they faced were very, very difficult indeed." In the camps this included being scrubbed with brushes hard enough to tear off skin and other tortures. "They would be prodded with bayonets, both on their body and in their eyes. Sometimes they would have ropes tied around their necks and be pulled around. In some cases they were dunked into big pits of manure. They were beaten."

Despite being reviled and abused for their stance at the time, many of those in various countries who had opposed the war, including Conscientious Objectors, became influential in public life in the decades afterwards. In 1935, for instance, New Zealander Mark Briggs was personally approached by the country's first Labour prime minister, Michael Joseph Savage, and asked if he would stand for a seat in the parliamentary upper house, the Legislative Council. David Grant says Savage wanted Briggs to serve as "a conscience to the folly of war. Briggs initially said no, he didn't think he was worthy of that honour. Savage asked him three times." Finally Briggs agreed, was elected and served for 16 years.

In Britain, says Cyril Pearce, some COs found it difficult to get jobs after the war, but others made important contributions to politics, from local council level up. Across Britain in the 1920s and '30s, "you see increasing numbers of former conscientious objectors being elected to high office".

Perhaps Australia's most notable example of a vocal anti-war campaigner rising to public prominence was

John Curtin. During 1916 Curtin travelled from town to town speaking against Hughes's conscription referendum. Despite its defeat he, along with other eligible men, was ordered to report for military training. Curtin refused and was arrested and jailed. Such was the outcry from Labor supporters, he was released three days later. In 1928 he began his first stint in Australia's federal parliament when he won the seat of Fremantle.

As World War II began Curtin affirmed his opposition to conscription, a position he maintained when he became prime minister in 1941. However, two years later, following the fall of Singapore and after many bitter debates, he finally gave in to pressure and introduced a limited version of conscription for overseas service, earning the condemnation of many in his own party. An exhibition produced by the John Curtin Prime Ministerial Library on the life of Curtin (who, poignantly, died in office just six weeks shy of World War II's end in 1945) says no decision in his entire public life caused him to do more soul-searching.

5

HELL AND HEALING

How did the medical profession rise to the challenge of so many wounded?

The ambulance vehicles servicing the advanced dressing stations almost always have to traverse roads exposed to shell fire, if not rifle fire … Hour after hour and sometimes for weeks there is a constant inflow of stretcher-borne men …

— "The Royal Army Medical Corps and Its Work",
British Medical Journal, 1917

The years before World War I had been characterised in many parts of the world by scientific and medical progress. Huge leaps had been made in understanding the nature of infection and in developing more effective treatments for all kinds of medical conditions. New hospitals were the modern marvels. And recent conflicts such as the Second Boer War had provided valuable experience to doctors in the field. So when World War I began the authorities thought they knew what to expect and were prepared to deal with it.

It didn't take long for the harsh truth to be revealed: this war damaged people in ways never seen before, on a scale previously unimagined, even by hardened military surgeons. Doctors, nurses and lowly stretcher-bearers had to adapt incredibly quickly under extreme duress. The inspiring way they did so led to breakthroughs we still benefit from today.

There were different problems to be faced across all the different environments in which the war was waged: the steamy tropics, the arid deserts, the frozen steppes. But it was the new trench warfare on the Western Front that delivered some of the biggest medical challenges. Ashley Ekins, co-editor of *War Wounds: Medicine and the Trauma of Conflict*, says that in thinking back to World War I, "Most people still have images of soldiers with rifles and bayonets, and of course they were equipped that way. But a very small proportion of wounds were ever perpetrated with bayonets, for example." Instead, more than three-quarters of the injuries were caused by high-velocity rifle bullets or shrapnel from artillery. This produced "wounds ghastly beyond any previous comprehension".

It was a shock to the system of medicos who had served in previous wars, says Dr Emily Mayhew, author of *Wounded: From Battlefield to Blighty, 1914–1918*. "The ones that were in the Boer War had good experience of casualty; they'd been fairly far forward, they'd done work on wounded men, but seven out of 10 men in the hospitals in the Boer War had diseases rather than wounds. Between the end of the Boer War and the beginning of the Great War there had been seismic shifts in technology — the power of guns, the size of artillery, the ability to damage a human form — and they'd simply never seen anything like it."

None of it was simple, or predictable. On the one hand, Emily Mayhew says, there were "great holes blown in people that went in very deep, that took in dirt and ragged pieces of uniform"; on the other, there was seemingly innocuous surface damage that hid deadly injuries. "They would get a man on the operating table and he would have a small nick, a centimetre's worth of cut. They would open him up and find that the bullet had gone in and done horrific damage and there was nothing they could do." Within weeks it was clear they needed a whole new approach.

One doctor forced into a new way of thinking was Scottish surgeon Henry Souttar. He'd had plenty of experience of the newly modernised London teaching hospitals, fitted out with white-tiled operating theatres featuring banks of lights, state-of-the-art sterilisers and new surgical instruments. So he felt right at home when he was posted to the well-equipped, well-staffed, 150-bed Belgian Field Hospital in Antwerp soon after the outbreak of hostilities. But within weeks the German army advanced on Antwerp and besieged the city. The hospital staff made it out just before Antwerp fell on 10 October.

Souttar and Dr Henry Munro, who had equipped an ambulance corps for Belgium, decided to band together. After a perilous evacuation they ended up in what Mayhew calls "the last unoccupied corner of Belgium", Furnes (now called Veurne), near the frontline of the Ypres Salient. Here Souttar and Munro set up base in a monastery-turned-school. Their "No. 1 Belgian Field Hospital" had Souttar running a staff of eight doctors and around two dozen nurses, with some of the school's professors volunteering as orderlies.

Here, Mayhew says, Souttar "discovered that actually he didn't need his very posh operating theatre, he didn't need the lights, he didn't need the tiling. He needed to be ready to operate, he needed a team that would support him, and most of all he needed to be as close to the point of wounding as possible."

In his vivid memoir *A Surgeon in Belgium*, Souttar describes receiving 350 casualties in the first four days at Furnes, "all of them with injuries of the most terrible nature". The proximity to battle might have been forced upon him, but he was quick to grasp its significance: the speed with which he could treat patients made up for the lack of modern equipment. Says Mayhew, he found that if he got in quickly and repaired the venous damage and the abdominal injuries and set the bone fractures, "he would save more lives than he would have if he'd been in his fully equipped hospital".

Individuals were gaining knowledge fast, and so were medical corps, sharing information across national boundaries. From their French colleagues British surgeons picked up debriding techniques, which meant getting to the very bottom of a wound and removing all the dead or contaminated tissue and any foreign matter. This gave the wounds a much better chance of healing and gave the surgeons more treatment options. Mayhew says early in the war, before this development, British doctors were "amputating pretty much anything that came in, any serious damage to what they call locomotive function in a limb". Debriding brought significant improvement, allowing them to "do as much conservative surgery as possible".

Doctors weren't the only ones who were learning. Mayhew says that one of the most overlooked roles in the entire war is that of the stretcher-bearers. In fact the only official war history that even mentions them is Australia's. "They don't get a mention in the British official history or the Canadian, but the Australians give them a paragraph." And yet, she says, their work was vital.

Their job underwent a remarkable and speedy transformation in response to the confronting realities of the new style of warfare. Initially, Mayhew says, stretcher-bearers were largely the men who played in military bands. "Or men considered, and this is a quote, 'Too big or too stupid to do proper soldiering'. They had no training. They were really porters, expected to pick up the wounded and bring them to a doctor where medical treatment would begin."

But just as a new approach had been forced on Souttar and the other doctors, it became obvious, to the British at least, that this old way of dealing with the injured simply would not work. A new bearer corps was quickly recruited and trained, becoming the forerunner of today's paramedics.

The training began with a six-week course in London, in which the bearers learned first-responder medical skills and underwent intensive fitness training. On Box Hill, which tested the mettle of the Olympic road cyclists in 2012, they spent hours practising carrying heavily laden stretchers up and down without dropping their loads. Then they were shipped to France, where they were assigned to a regimental medical officer who taught them other essential skills such as how to prevent haemorrhage.

Courage was an essential part of the job. While the soldiers were readying themselves at the front of a trench, awaiting the order to go over the top, the unarmed bearers were at the back with their big wooden stretchers, trying, says Mayhew, to be as invisible as possible because the fighting men often considered them unlucky. "They'd jostle them and say, 'Why don't you get a rifle? Why don't you do some fighting?' There's none of the adrenaline and the team spirit that the soldiers have as they go out on the top." The sound the bearers listened for wasn't enemy fire, it was the cries of the wounded.

Once they had found a wounded man, the bearers' work had only just begun. If they got very lucky they could load up their casualty and make it back to the relative safety of the trench. But if the shell-fire or rifle-fire was heavy, they would look for the nearest deep shell-hole or whatever other cover they could find. Here, pinned down by sniper fire, artillery fire or both, they would have to administer any treatment they could.

When they judged the risk to have lessened sufficiently they would set out with their heavy load. "By which time," says Mayhew, "the landscape has been transformed, it's been blasted to pieces. The trench network that they knew is gone. They have to find a way to get back to an aid post. The aid post itself may be gone. And so they are having to improvise every step of the way." And, she adds, they did this in mud, rain and snow.

They also had to learn to manage the patient. One of the trickiest things was holding off giving morphine, even though the man might have been crying out in agony. Mayhew explains that "It's much easier if they don't give morphine to someone on the way back to the aid post. If they have morphine the patient becomes a dead weight — they can't tell you what hurts, they can't tell you if they've started bleeding again, and it makes it difficult for morphine or any other analgesic or anaesthetic to be administered once they're in the field hospital."

What the stretcher-bearers did instead, she says, was to develop a manner that transcended the chaos around them. "They would say, 'We're nearly there, you'll get morphine when we get to the aid post', and it worked. "They learned to keep people calm just by the sound of their voices and by their own confidence and their own dedication. That's a very considerable skill. It's difficult to write about in a medical journal, but keeping somebody on as low a painkiller as possible is a life-saving skill. It's one that these men — who didn't come from medical school backgrounds, they were generally working-class men — learned."

The doctors to whom they delivered the patients quickly recognised this, and the weekly training sessions became a two-way exchange. Doctors would show the stretcher-bearers medical techniques and the bearers would in turn teach the doctors how to coach a patient through without morphine.

This non-hierarchical flow of information was characteristic of the medical personnel on the Western Front — unlike other theatres of the war, says Mayhew. Surgeons, for instance, were continually adapting to the new challenges, figuring out what worked and what didn't. "They adjust and change, and they know they can't really do this if they're going to stay within traditional authority structures. So it becomes much more of a team effort. They have all sorts of conferences and small newsletters that they circulate to each other to pass on the knowledge they've found. They're not sending everything back to a central organisation. They have quite an independent medical system out there sharing knowledge without worrying about what London thinks."

Among the many medical advances made during the war, perhaps the best known were those in plastic surgery. Again, these were breakthroughs made through two-fold necessity: first, trenches protected bodies, but lifting your eyes to see what was happening made the face and head very vulnerable, and second, to the initial amazement of surgeons, men survived with horrendous wounds, from having their nose shot off to having their whole face ripped off by shrapnel.

New Zealand-born, British-trained ear, nose and throat surgeon Harold Gillies saw these wounds first-hand serving with the Royal Army Medical Corps in France in 1915. Back in England the following year he set up a dedicated ward for maxillofacial injuries (those to the face, jaws and neck) at the Cambridge Military Hospital in Aldershot, London. Expecting 200 patients from the Battle of the Somme, the ward received 2,000. Gillies successfully argued that a purpose-built hospital was needed for such cases, and in 1917 the Queen's Hospital (now Queen Mary's Hospital) opened in Sidcup, Kent. Here Gillies and other specialists from around the Commonwealth treated 5,000 men injured in the war.

Kerry Neale has studied the work of Gillies, among others, for her PhD "Without the Faces of Men", which examines the treatment of facial wounds and the ongoing impacts on the men of these injuries. Techniques were continually being developed and refined at Sidcup and, she says, the results were remarkable, particularly in light of the limitations; there was, for instance, no blood crossmatching for the blood transfusions that were given, and most crucially of all there were no antibiotics. Infection was a huge risk.

Skin grafts had been recorded in India as far back as 800 BCE. Gillies read up on this and everything else he could find, adapting and refining as he went, until he was able to successfully take a section of rib cartilage and implant it in the forehead of a man whose nose had been blown off. Attached to blood vessels and then sealed under the skin, it could safely heal until it was strong enough to be swung into position, still attached at one end (and therefore still getting its blood supply) to form a new nose. A process like this could take three or four years, but the results were extraordinary.

Some of these innovations, developed through trial and error in urgent circumstances by Gillies and his colleagues, are still being used today. The tube pedicle is one. This was a brilliant response to the problem of skin-graft infections. It involved partially cutting away a section of flesh from an uninjured part of the body which was close to the wound — the chest, say, for someone with a face wound. Rather than completely cut out the area which would become the graft, it would be loosened into a flap which retained an anchor point, where it was still attached to its original blood vessels. It would then be rolled into a tube with the skin on the outside. The loose end of the tube would be attached to blood vessels in the place where the graft was needed. The living, blood-fed tissue inside the tube would be given natural protection by the layer of skin until the new connection had successfully taken. The anchor point could then be cut and the flesh could be unrolled and surgically attached to repair the wound.

To unaccustomed eyes, these patients presented a nightmarish sight: both the original injuries and the tube pedicles and other repairs in progress. It took a very special group of nurses to care for them, cleaning wounds, feeding men with gaping holes where their mouths should be, keeping them from despair. Unlike the doctors, many of these women are unknown to us, their details lost to time. However, Neale says that Gillies had no doubt about the worth of this group, whom he referred to as his "amazons".

"Mirrors were banned in the wards altogether," she says. "But of course that doesn't stop the men from looking around at the other patients and doing a bit of 'Well, if I'm as bad as him this is where my life will take me, but at least I'm not as bad as the gentleman two beds down.'" They also watched keenly for the reactions of the nurses. The nurses spoke privately of their trepidation when they were unwrapping the bandages, particularly at the very end of the treatment. While a man was still in the process of having his face reconstructed there was hope, "but when he'd gone through that final operation, how were they going to look at these patients knowing that that was pretty much as good as it was going to get?"

Neale says that not only did these nurses have to do all the hard physical labour that comes with the job and control their own reactions to the things that confronted them every day, they also had to build the men up psychologically "to be able to go back out into the world". Doing so month after month, year after year, shows extraordinary resilience.

The men Gillies treated were, very understandably, suffering a psychological reaction to a physical injury, but a different kind of psychological reaction became one of the greatest medical challenges of the war — something labelled "shell shock".

Professor Edgar Jones, co-author of *Shell Shock to PTSD: Military Psychiatry from 1900 to the Gulf War*, says that the term emerged in the winter of 1914–15. It was first used by soldiers to describe how they felt when they were exposed to artillery fire. "So it doesn't begin as a recognised medical diagnosis. It's only when Charles Myers, consulting psychologist to the British Expeditionary Force, uses the term in *The Lancet* in February 1915 that it gets official recognition. Once it's forced its way into formal medical diagnosis, the armed forces have to take it seriously and they have to work out ways of treating it and understanding what this disorder is."

Understanding it was trickier than it might seem to us, with the benefit of hindsight. Initially, says Jones, the authorities thought it was a form of concussion or some kind of toxic exposure from an exploding shell. But they soon realised "that most soldiers who are breaking down with what is called 'shell shock' haven't necessarily been rendered unconscious. It's increasingly seen as the psychological pressure of warfare; that brave men are gradually worn down."

Soon enough shell shock became "a catch-all term for any disorder where they can't find a recognised medical disease — it could be chest pain, it could be difficulty breathing, it could be muscle pain, joint pain. All these symptoms are gathered together and described as shell shock because that's a very convenient way of describing soldiers who can't do their job on the battlefield but haven't been wounded and don't have a recognised disease." Ashley Ekins adds, "We know it far better from later conflicts as combat fatigue, battle exhaustion. It's completely reinvented for every conflict, in fact, but it's the same thing."

Jones says we have only estimates of how many people were affected but, taking British servicemen alone, between 200,000 and 300,000 had some form of "functional somatic disorder", in other words, physical symptoms without any identifiable physical cause.

Figuring out how to deal with these men was a work in progress. Jones says the British Army didn't have clinical psychologists at the time, "not because there was negligence, but because they just simply weren't expecting this". Since the army lacked other options, shell-shock patients were sent to base hospitals in France and if they didn't improve were sent to hospitals in Britain. But as the war went on the doctors treating these men realised that very few of them who reached the UK made a full recovery. As Henry Souttar had learned with physical damage, speed of treatment was key.

Charles Myers, the British Army's consulting psychologist, looked at how other armies were handling the problem, and in December 1916 instituted a system borrowed from the French; something Jones describes as "forward psychiatry", which meant providing treatment facilities as close to the battlefield as possible (Germany set up something similar the following year). "Myers set up four shell-shock units within about 10 to 20 miles of the frontline. This is ultimately called the PIE system: Proximity, Immediacy and Expectancy of recovery. It's a very quick, easy system; it's sleep, reassurance, good-quality food and then graduated exercise, in the hope that the man will get better within a week or two, with encouragement and rest."

The effectiveness of the PIE approach has been proven, says Jones. "Estimates from the Second World War, for example, suggested that 30 per cent of servicemen treated using PIE methods go back to active duty. It remains one of the key interventions of the military. It's used in Afghanistan, it was used in Iraq."

However, he says, it's important to look behind the statistics on the treatment of shell-shock patients to make sure we see the real picture. For instance, according to a purely statistical reading, 1918 saw a great many shell-shock patients get well enough to be discharged from military hospitals. But Jones says, "This wasn't because the doctors had had a big breakthrough in understanding psychological trauma." Rather, it was a pragmatic acceptance by authorities of the status quo.

"By 1918 they knew that a serviceman with chronic shell shock was very unlikely to go back to the frontline, but he was occupying a valuable bed in the medical system. So they passed a regulation that if a soldier got better he could be discharged from the armed forces." The treating doctors were then encouraged to say to their charges, "If you get better you can leave the army and you can get a much better paid job in a munitions factory or working on the land." "But it had to be done surreptitiously," says Jones; "it was never done publicly, because if a soldier fighting in the trenches heard that his cousin or brother had been discharged from the armed forces for shell shock, it would damage his morale."

As well as those suffering shell shock, there were the soldiers who took sometimes drastic action in order to get away from the fighting. This took various forms, says Ekins, right across the spectrum, from men feigning illnesses of various kinds to those who permanently disfigured themselves. They took a big risk doing this — if their actions were discovered they would be court-martialled.

Ekins describes one technique involving a .303 cartridge: "Very easy to do for a soldier. Pull the bullet out, take a strand of cordite and chew that. It used to raise the temperature, apparently, and give the symptoms of fever." Another technique was to inject petrol or paraffin into their knees and elbows to try to induce the symptoms of synovitis and tenosynovitis. But this was easily detected, he says. "Doctors would simply make a small incision and they'd smell the offending material straight away."

In fact doctors became very skilled at discerning who was genuinely unfit and who was "malingering", as it was known. But many of them were troubled by having to cross the line from treatment to coercion. "On the one hand they are there to maintain the manpower and strength, the fighting efficiency of the force, to keep men fit. But here they were, having to perhaps send men for a very severe prison sentence if they found them out," says Ekins.

Some soldiers took more drastic action than chewing cordite or injecting paraffin. "Men would shoot off a foot or a finger in order to escape the line," he says. There were giveaway signs that these injuries were self-inflicted: "There'd be powder burns, the rifle was so close." But some doctors responded compassionately, realising these men were at breaking point. "They knew that some of them had been very good soldiers but had just come to the end of their tether." They simply chose not to report soldiers they knew had shot themselves. Others went a step further: in researching his book *War Wounds* Ekins found one doctor who demonstrated how to apply iodine to get rid of the powder burn.

The war profoundly affected all who experienced it. Millions of survivors were irreparably damaged physically or mentally. But for others the war provided inspiration that would blossom many years later. Henry Souttar went on to become a highly influential figure in British medicine. He was knighted in 1949 in recognition of his many contributions, one of which was his pioneering work in the development of what we now call radiotherapy. Souttar was already deeply interested in physics before the war, but an unexpected encounter he had at the Furnes field hospital galvanised that interest.

His surprise visitor was French scientist Marie Curie, who had already won Nobel Prizes in both Physics and Chemistry, and had made huge leaps forward in possible diagnostic applications for x-rays, which had been discovered 20 years earlier. Hearing reports about the damage being caused by shrapnel and the difficulties surgeons were having finding the tiny fragments, Curie had become determined to do something to help. She bought a van, learned to drive it, and adapted it to serve as a mobile radiology lab, the first in what would become a little fleet, staffed by her lab assistants.

Emily Mayhew says that Curie understood that the new weapons required new methods of treatment, and that being able to take x-rays in the most forward position possible could make a huge difference to the outcome of surgery. Practical and resourceful, she thought of everything, even inventing a special pen that could write on the x-ray film. But generating the idea and funding the equipment weren't enough. At age 47, this extraordinary woman got into her van, drove herself to the field hospitals close to the frontlines and offered her services.

Not everyone at every hospital was appreciative. "Some of the surgeons say, 'I won't have a woman in my operating theatre, doesn't matter if she *has* got a Nobel Prize!'" says Mayhew. Not so Souttar, who was well aware of Curie and a great admirer of her work. "He's rendered speechless when she arrives," says Mayhew. "His heroine has turned up and he thinks it's just fantastic. She rigs up her little van and she takes films of the soldiers who come in with multiple fragments of shell in them, prints up the films and then takes them around immediately into theatre so that she and the surgeons can look for these little pieces of metal."

The work of Curie and her team saved many lives, perhaps thousands, says Mayhew — healing amid the hell.

6

THE PEN AND THE SWORD

Why do the British "war poets" dominate battle literature?

This is the young men's year!
They are gone, one and all, at duty's call,
To the camp, to the trench, to the sea.
They have left their homes, they have left their all,
And now, in ways heroical,
They are making history.

— From "In Church, 1916" by John Oxenham

When you think of the writing that emerged from World War I what's the first thing that comes to mind — The poems of Wilfred Owen, perhaps, with their images of the guns' monstrous anger and men dying in mustard-gas agony? Chances are high that it is the work of Owen or of fellow Briton Siegfried Sassoon that springs up; this has come to be the prism through which we see the war. But if they had been asked the same question between 1914 and 1918, or even in the two decades afterwards, readers across the English-speaking world would have given quite different answers. People outside the English written tradition still would today.

Dr Christina Spittel is a lecturer in English at the University of New South Wales (Canberra) and is writing a book on the treatment of the war in Australian fiction. She points out that Owen — killed in battle in Ors, France, in November 1918, just a week before the war ended — remained little known for many years after his death. Only decades later was he raised from literary obscurity, by which time the poets who were prominent during the war years were almost entirely forgotten.

A prime example of the latter is John Oxenham, a pseudonym of prolific English writer William Arthur Dunkerley. Oxenham wrote "very consoling, very conservative poetry" which carried an explicit religious message: everything that happened, even the loss of young men in war, was meaningful and worthwhile. "That was an important message that some people who were grieving and people who were worried about their next of kin needed and wanted to hear during the war years," Spittel says. It's hard to overstate Oxenham's popularity in his day. His "Hymn for Men at the Front" sold in the millions, as did special editions of his poems designed to fit in a uniform pocket. Yet now, "I think he doesn't even make it into *The Cambridge Companion to the Literature of the First World War*, poor man," she says.

Vincent Sherry agrees that talking about the war by focusing solely on writers such as Owen, Sassoon and Germany's Erich Maria Remarque gives an incomplete picture of the times. Professor Sherry, author of *The Great War and the Language of Modernism* and editor of the self-same *Cambridge Companion to the Literature of the First World War*, says, "There is a tendency to read history backwards; to read the whole war from the vantage point of 1918 and the accumulated woe and maim and colossal atrocity that we now know it to have been." But to do so is to forget that it began on a far different note, with both established authors and those the war would make famous, such as Rupert Brooke, patriotically supporting it.

Governments on both sides were quick to harness this support, says Sherry. British, French and German leaders sought out writers to, in effect, "consecrate the cause; they had a cultural authority". In England, within weeks of the commencement of hostilities, 24 literary powerhouses of the day, including Thomas Hardy, J.M. Barrie, G.K. Chesterton, John Masefield, H.G. Wells and John Galsworthy, gathered around a table in Whitehall, where they were asked to provide a cultural lead for their nation by "writing about and providing a reason for this war".

Then there was Brooke, who had already travelled widely and had published a collection of poetry by the time he voluntarily took up a naval commission at age 27, soon after the war began. He had mixed with the Bloomsbury group and was known in certain literary circles, but his work was only just starting to gain wider recognition when he died in April 1915 of septicaemia from a mosquito bite while en route to Gallipoli.

Brooke's passing came just weeks before the publication of his collection *1914 & Other Poems*, whose resolute idealism in the face of death resonated strongly with contemporary readers; it sold out reprint after reprint. The opening lines of "The Soldier" are still among the most memorable in British poetry: "If I should die, think only this of me; / That there's some corner of a foreign field / That is for ever England."

Yet even though Brooke's words live on, qualifying him as one of the best known British "war poets", it is not his view that characterises the war for readers a century later, but rather the ironic and bitter perspective expressed by Owen and Sassoon of war as a futile and wasteful exercise.

Owen's "Dulce et Decorum Est", for instance, details the grotesque suffering of a soldier too slow with his gas mask, and contrasts that ugly reality with the high ideals of those who send young men into battle. The poem is, says Sherry, "a cry against the politicos who have framed the war in terms of the Latin motto that Horace supposedly heard on the steps of the Capitol when a woman who had lost her seventh son in one of the wars said, '*Dulce et decorum est pro patria mori*' — 'It is sweet and honourable to die for one's country'." This is a sentiment in keeping with Brooke's work, but Owen fiercely rejects it, calling it "the old lie".

So what happened to bring the Owen–Sassoon view to the fore, to make theirs the dominant voices in the canon of World War I literature? The Vietnam War, for one thing. "Canons aren't stable things that we unearth at a big archaeological dig," says Spittel. "Canons are shaped by our own concerns, our interests, our own views about the world ... The big names we associate with that literature today, Wilfred Owen, Siegfried Sassoon and so on, are names that became really important in the 1960s and '70s."

A generation shaped by "the dramatic and traumatic experience of Vietnam" and the huge anti-war movements this sparked around the world found something in these poems that spoke to them, says Spittel. So much so that the generation which newly discovered the work of these soldier-writers granted it a significance beyond artistic expression: "Their poetry comes to stand as almost a historical document." Dr Ann-Marie Einhaus, author of *The Short Story and the First World War* and co-editor of *The Penguin Book of First World War Stories*, says there's another dynamic at work too: despite the detail of trenches and gassings, this poetry, particularly Owen's, is "sufficiently universal that you can relate other wars to it. It's become the stand-in for suffering in war *per se*, not just suffering in the First World War."

There were several key critics who brought these poets to wide attention. The first two were British — Bernard Bergonzi and Jon Silkin. Bergonzi, who was Professor of English at the University of Warwick, led the way in 1965 with *Heroes' Twilight*, a study of the literature the war had produced. Silkin, who was himself a poet as well as founder of the influential poetry magazine *Stand*, championed the work of Owen, Isaac Rosenberg and others in his 1972 book *Out of Battle* and in several anthologies. Bergonzi and Silkin established the canon as we know it, says Sherry, and it then caught the interest of American literary scholar Paul Fussell.

Fussell "inherited that canon and waved a wand over it and revealed how wonderful this writing was," says Sherry. But the writing he valued was "of a single partisan stripe. For him, what mattered was the intelligence, the coherence, the wit of the objection to war." Fussell's privileged background hadn't prevented him from being drafted into service in 1943. Fighting in Europe, he earned the Bronze Star and two Purple Hearts, and while he wrote many years later of the "salutary" effect the experience had had on him, he also described war's visceral horror and was scathing of high-minded attempts to justify it.

For someone who declared, as Fussell did, that every war was ironic "because every war is worse than expected", the satire and sharp criticism in the work of writers such as Sassoon, Owen and Robert Graves made their voices entirely relevant seven decades later.

In what is often described as a landmark work, 1975's *The Great War and Modern Memory*, Fussell demonstrated how the altered nature of warfare had changed the tropes and imagery used by its writers. Dawn, for instance, had been employed as a symbol of hope for thousands of years, but for the soldiers of World War I daylight often brought despair because it meant renewed attack. The new technology of airplanes provided another example, as Sherry explains: "Before the war they were images of fantasy and release and romance and by the end of the war they were demonised: they were dropping bombs, they were dropping mustard gas. That image changed totally."

Christina Spittel says it's not only what these writers were saying that drew Fussell to them, but also how they were saying it. "If you are writing literary history you're looking for writers who push the boundaries of literary expression, and people like Wilfred Owen and Siegfried Sassoon did precisely that. They were writing modernist poetry. They are technically innovative and they're trying to do something new, whereas our friend John Oxenham did not. He was writing poetry which, from the perspective of literary history, is boring; it's 19th century, it's all been said before, it's all been done before."

Sherry points out that between the idealism of Brooke at the beginning of the war and the disillusionment of Owen and Sassoon at the end of it came a great deal worth noting. "What's in the middle is a literature of record, a literature of experience, a literature that is not so much interested in political position, a literature of the day-by-day of it." He nominates poets Ivor Gurney, Edward Thomas and Isaac Rosenberg as writers who were "just trying to get through it". They weren't attempting to formulate an opinion on the war as a whole, but rather to capture their experience of it.

He also notes that while the poetry tended to be published during the war (or, like Owen's posthumous 1920 volume, soon after), prose needed to be "ripened and gestated" and took longer. So while there were isolated but noteworthy examples such as C.E. Montague's *Disenchantment*, published in 1922, it wasn't until the late 1920s that a surge of British memoirs and novels about the war appeared, including Graves's memoir *Good-Bye to All That* in 1929 and Sassoon's novel *Memoirs of an Infantry Officer* the following year.

What Sherry describes as "one of the most interesting accounts of the war" first appeared in 1929 under the title *The Middle Parts of Fortune*, attributed to "Private 19022" but really the work of Australian-born, British-based Frederic Manning. An expurgated version, *Her Privates We*, came out the following year to acclaim from Ernest Hemingway and others — in fact, says Sherry, Hemingway later said of it, "That is the book I read once a year no matter what, to remind me of what it was really like."

Hemingway had, of course, seen the war at first hand, volunteering as an ambulance driver in Italy. His 1929 novel *A Farewell to Arms* is the best-known example of the American literature of World War I, although, Sherry says, "his own war experience was very much exaggerated by him". Unsurprisingly, American works are very different to the British and European literature of the period. While in many British accounts, the war marks an end — of empire or of British invulnerability — American writers tend to characterise it as the beginning of world-power status. "The notion is that the Yanks came in late and last, but they take all the credit. Whatever truth there may be to that, they really were in the war for less than a year, in effect. And their losses were nothing like the losses for the British. It is not a marker on the landscape of history in this country the way it is in Britain or in Canada or Australia," Missouri-based Sherry says.

Erich Maria Remarque's novel *All Quiet on the Western Front* had also appeared in English translation in 1929, just months after its German publication. Sherry describes it as "a singular book in the level of its outrage and its indignation. It was an exception, but it struck a chord and it seems to have tapped this reservoir of anger and disillusion that many of those who had fought really experienced."

Ann-Marie Einhaus says the disillusionment of soldiers on their return home was also a significant factor in the skewing of the World War I literary canon toward cynicism.

In the works of fiction produced while the war was still taking place, modernist writers such as D.H. Lawrence tried to broadly reflect on its psychological effects, but for others it was more or less colourful window-dressing: "So we have romance, we have spy tales that used to be perhaps mystery thrillers, detective stories, comic stories which basically just adopt a wartime setting and wartime heroes. What better thing for a romance writer than to put a man in uniform in the story?"

These bluff, resourceful heroes continued to appear after the war, with the enormously popular "Bulldog Drummond" novels by Sapper, aka H.C. McNeile, being a prime example. Having been an officer in the trenches of the Western Front (as McNeile himself was), Drummond finds peace so tedious that he advertises himself as a kind of gentleman adventurer in *The Times*. There were plenty of other, lesser-known characters along similar lines, says Einhaus. "We have a lot of detective tough men coming back and using their wartime skills. They have very little patience for the civilian who stayed at home and maybe made a career for himself."

At the same time, she says, there were writers with more literary leanings in whom the war provoked very different feelings. Richard Aldington is one. Aldington was also an officer on the Western Front, but unlike McNeile he was traumatised by the experience and unable to settle into post-war life. In 1929 he published what Einhaus describes as "a very bitter novel about the war, *Death of a Hero*. He also wrote a volume of short stories, many of them very scathing, about the experience of the returned veteran. The experience of returning home expecting to be going back into a good job, expecting to be welcomed with open arms, and then finding yourself in the middle of economic depression where other people have taken your job and there's just not that need for your talents — all of that hugely contributed to this idea of the war as futile."

There was limited appreciation of these kinds of anti-war messages in the immediate post-war period. Much of the detail recollected or fictionalised by those who had been there was considered simply too harsh for the public to bear. Books in both Britain and America were censored at their government's behest or were pre-emptively altered by their publishers or authors. Hemingway, Remarque and Manning all suffered such expurgation, as did Aldington — who protested against it by insisting that his British publishers, Chatto & Windus, insert asterisks to indicate the omissions.

Recalling Owen's image of a gassed soldier flung onto a wagon in agony and the way such images would have been received by the relatives of those who served, Spittel comments, "that's hardly something people wanted to hear". But Einhaus refers to historian Dan Todman's observation that by the 1960s many of these relatives had died off, and the younger generation was more willing to absorb the details of the horrors of war and so, she says, "it was suddenly possible to take this very negative view in a way that maybe it wasn't possible earlier".

The futile, soul-destroying view of the war is one that has remained prevalent, even in the works of authors born long after the events they are describing, says Einhaus. "Something that strikes me about more recent fiction about the First World War is that it seems to be getting more and more miserable. Novels like Helen Dunmore's *The Lie* or another recent one, John Boyne's *The Absolutist*, are really depressing. It's quite interesting to think why people might be craving this sort of extreme, negative view of the war at a time where they're also very much celebrating achievements or sacrifice. I think there's a certain contradictory nature there to how we remember the war, certainly in Britain today. On the one hand there's the feeling that these men died for us — they died for a good cause in a certain sense; they have to be honoured. On the other hand, there's this myth of complete futility that seems to be perpetuated in these new books."

Einhaus adds that while there certainly were writers who experienced the war and saw themselves as part of a generation lost to it, including Vera Brittain who wrote about her war experiences nursing in England and France in the memoir *Testament of Youth*, "I suspect it's something that a lot of people who lived through the war would not necessarily have agreed with."

Spittel concurs, and offers the example of Australian writer Leonard Mann and his self-published 1932 novel *Flesh in Armour*. She says that Mann, who died in 1981, was haunted until the end of his life by his experiences on the Western Front, including being buried alive in a trench by a shell blast, yet the book presents a nuanced picture. "In his novel you've got very different characters and each character has a very different experience of the war. You've got someone who really finds his purpose — who really makes this work for him, who is at home amongst the men, who enjoys the mateship. This environment which eventually will kill him is an environment that is not threatening his morale or his psychic wellbeing. At the other extreme you've got a character who ends up committing suicide and who puts down his stripes because he can no longer command his men. That's a novel, for me, that speaks something about the truth of the war because it tries to capture that the war meant different things to different people."

There are plenty of commentators who will argue that writers like Mann have remained obscure while Owen and Sassoon and Graves have dominated the World War I canon purely because of the quality of their work — its enduring literary value. Spittel says it's not so simple. "I'm a bit sceptical about enduring literary value. I think literary values are also constructs of their time. I think *Flesh in Armour* is still very fresh, it still speaks to us. (It has just been reprinted and here in Australia it's available in the shops for the first time in about 20 years, and it's really worth reading.) So I don't think it's just that." Novels that treat the war as a big imperialist adventure have faded from view as our world-view has changed, says Spittel. "They no longer speak to us because we can no longer conceive of going to war for an imperial cause." Such novels have, she says, dated in a way that much of the poetry has not.

But one book that lives on despite, perhaps, being mistaken by some as a gung-ho take on war-as-adventure is *The Anzac Book*. Spittel explains that the book consists of writing and illustrations done on Gallipoli by the men who were serving there — despite the title, not just Australians but some from other parts of the empire too. "It was very much an imperial book with a strong emphasis on the Australian effort." The idea was to offer a diversion to the troops who were trapped in a stalemate, on an increasingly cold, wintry peninsula, having seen 10,000 of their brothers-in-arms die over the previous seven months.

It was edited by Charles Bean, Australia's official war correspondent and war historian. Spittel says its provenance was "a little bit exaggerated. Fewer men actually wrote in with their poems and their drawings than has been claimed." But it was an immediate hit, going out to the various countries in the empire and selling more than 100,000 copies in 1916 in Australia alone.

Despite its mass acceptance, the book is not all cheeky Aussie larrikinism and grudging respect for "Johnny Turk", as is sometimes assumed. "It is often remembered as the first crystallisation of the Anzac legend but if you look at it more closely, it's quite messy," says Spittel. "There were some darker voices in *The Anzac Book*." Bean did, however, feel the need to omit "some more critical voices". Examples of the contributions he rejected, including cartoons poking fun at British military brass, have been included in the current edition, produced under the imprimatur of the Australian War Memorial.

The passage of time has given us a different perspective on satirising generals. It has also made us aware of how many other voices and lives have been completely omitted from the literary canon of World War I. Dr Santanu Das, author of *Touch and Intimacy in First World War Literature* and editor of *The Cambridge Companion to the Poetry of the First World War*, explains. "More than four million non-white men were recruited into the armies of Europe and the United States during the First World War, but even today — that is, 100 years after its outbreak — we know less about them than about the four major British First World War poets."

Das says that in recent years the war's literary canon has expanded to accommodate "poetry by civilians like Thomas Hardy and Rudyard Kipling, or by women. For example, there's some excellent poetry by women poets such as Charlotte Mew and Rose Macaulay. But even now colonial poetry, particularly by non-white soldiers, is scarcely visible in the canon."

Seeking out these missing voices will help us come to grips with a basic but often overlooked truth about the war, he says: that it wasn't just confined to the Western Front or Anzac Cove. Discovering unfamiliar voices and the experiences they describe can broaden our horizons beyond the mud of Flanders. "For a very long time war literature has been conflated with trench poetry written by a handful of soldier-poets. That is fundamentally going to change," he says.

But this isn't a zero-sum game. Acknowledging other viewpoints does not mean discarding those currently in the canon. "I do not for a moment want to downplay the power of canonical war poetry," says Das. "Much of my own work has been on Wilfred Owen. When I was editing *The Cambridge Companion to the Poetry of the First World War* I wanted to recognise the enduring power of poets like Wilfred Owen, Siegfried Sassoon, or Isaac Rosenberg. But at the same time, it is absolutely essential to acknowledge the fact that First World War literature is far more international and far broader than that of the British trench lyric. It has to include European poets such as Giuseppe Ungaretti and August Stramm, and beyond to figures such as Rabindranath Tagore in India, Claude

McKay in the West Indies, Robert Service in Canada, or Katherine Mansfield who, after losing her brother in the war, wrote some of her most beautiful short stories, often drawing on their childhood in New Zealand."

The realisation that gaps existed has prompted the rediscovery of colonial war literature, such as the novel *Across the Black Waters* by India's Mulk Raj Anand, whose father worked in the Indian Army (though he was not mobilised). Although it was written in 1939, Das says it is very useful in reconstructing the South Asian experience of the war.

But to really capture the full picture, historians and other academics have to look beyond just what is written. "Most of the colonial soldiers were semi-literate or non-literate, recruited from poor, often village, backgrounds," says Das. "As a result they have not left us with a tremendous fund of short stories, poems, journals, memoirs that form the cornerstone of European or Australian or Canadian war memory. But being non-literate does not mean being non-literary. These men often came from communities with very strong oral cultures and they bring these traditions to France or to Mesopotamia all the way from India or Senegal. They bring with them their songs, their prayers, their stories."

Some of these were preserved courtesy of the fact that Allied prisoners of war, including a large number of South Asians, were kept in POW camps in Zossen and Wunsdorf, just south of Berlin, where, says Das, they were studied by a group of German academics: "The Royal Prussian Phonographic Commission made over 2,000 sound-recordings between 1915 and 1918." As well as these invaluable recordings of the South Asians, "we also have songs by French, Flemish, Welsh, Senegalese and Russian soldiers, among others." Then there was the music of those who stayed behind: "There are the most poignant laments sung by women in India after their men left." Nor was this oral tradition confined to the Entente side. "There's a substantial fund of songs from the Turkish soldiers and the women they had left behind."

Das says we need to stretch the way we think about the canon in order to include this wealth of material: "In the way that our idea of the war changed with our understanding that it was not confined to the trenches of the Western Front but also happened in Mesopotamia, Gallipoli, East Africa, Palestine, Egypt and Sinai, so must we change our idea of what constitutes its literature."

7

THE VIEW FROM BERLIN

How did the war unfold inside "enemy territory"?

Rashness and weakness are driving the world into the most frightful war, the ultimate aim of which is to destroy Germany.

— Kaiser Wilhelm II, 30 July 1914

In Chapter 1 we looked at the events that led up to the war, and the differing views then and in later years about where blame should fall. We learned a little about how the Central Powers — who were unquestionably the aggressors in the Allies' eyes — believed they were fighting a defensive war. Time, now, to delve deeper into the experience of those who would emerge as the war's losers: Germany, Austria-Hungary and the Ottoman Empire.

For Professor Ute Daniel, author of *The War from Within: German Women in the First World War*, the war provides a harsh and unforgettable lesson that "small things may have huge and unexpected consequences". The German and Austro-Hungarian leaders had pictured a battle they could control, one that would give them "a better position in the international pecking order"; instead they got a world war with death and destruction on an unprecedented scale.

Professor Gerhard Hirschfeld, whose many books include the co-authored *Scorched Earth: The Germans on the Somme 1914–1918*, feels that both Germany and Austria-Hungary could have taken steps to de-escalate the building tension after the assassination of Archduke Franz Ferdinand. But, he adds, "in my opinion it's very important to note that Germany and Austria-Hungary, as well as all the other countries involved in the diplomatic struggle, acted out of fear". Or rather, out of different fears — of losing their particular cultures, of losing their empires and of falling behind in the colonial race.

Hirschfeld says that there were some dissenting voices within Germany that wanted to see peace maintained, but they were overwhelmed by the politicians and military leaders who felt that war was "more or less inevitable", in which case they would be better off entering it sooner rather than later. "Looking at demography and industrial development within Russia, they said, 'This country is going to be so strong that after 1916 a war will be inevitable, so why not go to war in 1914 and then finish the business once and for all?'"

Germany's physical location also played into the pro-war mindset. "The question of *Einkreisen* — encirclement — became the dominant paradigm of German diplomats and military planners before the war," says Hirschfeld. "In 1906, then-Chancellor Bernhard von Bülow declared in a famous Reichstag speech at the German parliament that Germany felt encircled due to its geographic situation."

This reflected a major change which had begun soon after Wilhelm II ascended the throne in 1888. In the decades following the 1871 unification of Germany, the country's first leader, Chancellor Otto von Bismarck, worked very hard to maintain peace in Europe. He felt strongly that the security this provided for the new nation was far more important than expending effort trying to build up colonial holdings. He was also fiercely anti-socialist and in 1878 finally succeeded in having the popular Social Democratic Party banned.

But by 1890 Bismarck's ideas were looking very old-fashioned indeed to the new king, who pushed the 75-year-old statesman out, let the ban on socialism lapse and developed a *Weltpolitik* — foreign policy — which emphasised his own colonial ambitions and desire for naval power. He also allowed the treaty Bismarck had engineered with Russia to lapse, which led to Russia entering a pact with France. It was at this point that Russia began to pour money into building up its defences and industrial and military capability. In Germany itself the socialist movement grew and grew.

Hirschfeld says that "conservative elites" within Germany saw war as something that could deal with the growing unrest at home while expanding Germany's influence aboard. Their hope was "that a war involving all classes of society would help to undermine or perhaps even halt the apparently unstoppable rise of the social democratic workers' movement" while helping to fulfil the country's "oft-declared ambitions for colonies".

The enthusiasm for war wasn't limited to the power-wielding political and military elite within the country.

In fact, there was almost universal support for it, says Bernd Hüppauf, Professor Emeritus (retired) of German Literature and Literary Theory at New York University. Writers and other intellectuals joined in, along with the vast majority of the population, Hüppauf says. The outbreak of war triggered a wave of nationalistic fervour in which "not only established authors but hundreds of thousands of people engaged in writing poetry and sending it to the newspapers".

The population was united in believing that whatever else the war might achieve, it was a stand in defence of Germany's unique culture, a defence of an intellectual tradition "often associated with Romanticism that they felt had to be defended against both sides — against the West and its idea of civilisation and against Russia and Tsarist dictatorship". Even people who might have been expected to oppose the war were largely silent. "As an example, the Quakers were strong in America but almost absent on the continent, in Germany in particular," says Hüppauf.

But six months into the fighting, as autumn turned to winter, things began to change. Conditions got worse and worse for ordinary Germans and the population began to lose faith in its leaders. Belatedly they began to question what they had been told about the need for war. In May 1916 journalist and left-wing political activist Paul Frölich wrote a letter describing a gathering of almost 10,000 workers assembling in Berlin to protest the war. It was, he wrote, the first time such "open resistance" had occurred: "The ice was broken."

The workers were angry at the privations they and their families were suffering, notably lack of food. British ships had blockaded German ports, preventing supplies from being brought in that way, but that wasn't the sole cause of the problem, says Hirschfeld. "Food shortages were partly due to the British sea blockade, but also responsible was mishandling of food distribution within Germany." He says the German government could easily have blamed the British for the hunger and for the diseases resulting from this disastrous situation, but they didn't. Instead, the favoured propaganda approach was to maintain that Germany was succeeding on all fronts.

As well as food, other essential supplies were very scarce. A black market sprang up in response. "By 1917 almost one-third of German families were dependent on it," says Hirschfeld. "Even soldiers at the front were participating in it. We have letters from families to the soldiers asking them to provide necessary food and other materials which soldiers still could get at the front, but which were unavailable at home."

This put enormous pressure on women and their families, says Ute Daniel. "Food was in short supply. Meat, bread and clothes were very expensive, or only to be bought on the black market. And under these conditions, lots of townswomen turned to illegal methods for supporting their families. They made protest marches. They broke windows of magistrates and shopkeepers. They stole potatoes from the fields. And the youngsters, in lots of cases, were with them. That is to say, the teenagers and their mothers formed an alliance against the authorities. And in some instances the youngsters emancipated themselves completely from the family and did their own thing." It was, Hirschfeld says, "a breakdown in all parts of German society".

The suffering was captured in the work of artists and writers, some of them society's "outsiders" — schizophrenics and others locked away in mental institutions. These people, Hüppauf says, perished by the thousands as a result of malnutrition. "They were the last in the food chain and were not important so they just died of starvation." Many left behind artworks that show the reality of their situation, with turnips, the last food they would see, featuring prominently.

Hüppauf refers to a number of letters written by an Australian musician, Ethel Cooper, who was still living in Leipzig after the outbreak of war. Writing to her sister in Adelaide, Cooper "reported about the 'turnip winter' and felt that no one in Australia would be prepared to accept this kind of maltreatment of the population". If the same thing happened in Australia, Cooper speculated, it would cause a revolt.

There wasn't a revolt in Germany but there *was* a democratic attempt to bring an end to the war. On 6 July 1917 Centrist politician Matthias Erzberger called a parliamentary debate. In 1914 Erzberger had been an enthusiastic supporter of the war, advocating territorial expansion including full annexation of Belgium. But now, says Daniel, he told his fellow politicians "what nobody had dared to speak about before", namely that Germany's strategy of unrestricted submarine warfare wasn't working and had no chance of doing so. He urged his country to renounce all its annexation demands and to negotiate peace. Just under two weeks later, the motion passed in the Reichstag by a substantial majority. But the politicians were ignored by Wilhelm II and his military leaders, and brushed off by Georg Michaelis, the chancellor installed just days earlier by General Erich Ludendorff. So the suffering of ordinary Germans continued.

And what of Germany's fellow Central Powers nations — what was *their* experience of the war? Dr Marvin Fried, author of *Austro-Hungarian War Aims in the Balkans during World War I*, says that like Germany, Austria-Hungary did not imagine where its stance in July 1914 would lead. What Austria-Hungary wanted was to defend threats to its integrity, culminating in the assassination of the Archduke. "When it issued the ultimatum to Serbia and when it desired this conflict with Serbia, it never believed that it would result in a general European war."

Rather, the intended result was "a third Balkan war where Austria-Hungary would reverse the Serbian successes of the Second Balkan War and re-establish Austria-Hungary's authority in the Balkans". Fried describes Austria-Hungary as "an anachronistic empire"; unlike Germany or Russia, with their dominant central cores, it was a multinational entity. It felt the need to take aggressive steps to deal with what it saw as the Serbian threat because of the fear that a pan-nationalist movement of ethnic Serbs might gain momentum and set off a wave of attempted defections from the empire, "where the Italians want to secede, the Romanians want to secede, the Poles want to secede ..."

In 1914 Austria-Hungary was at the heart of Europe — its capital, Vienna, was famed as a centre of culture and intellectual life — yet four years later it no longer existed as such. "The country was a creative, advancing empire, an ancient one at that, and one in which science and culture flourished," Fried says. And yet the decisions its leaders made around the war would prove monumentally destructive.

"One of the answers can be found in the structure of the monarchy, which was complex to say the least." The "dual monarchy" system meant that while both Austria and Hungary maintained their own parliaments, the ruling Habsburg king–emperor appointed the prime ministers and cabinets for each, and all decisions were funnelled upward for royal approval. The arrangement was a uniquely complex one, says Fried, allowing "very few people to make some very key decisions that led to the outbreak of the war".

The decision to go to war might not have been made democratically in Austria-Hungary, but here, too, it received hearty public support. "The declaration of war was greeted with much popularity," says Fried. "Loyalty to the emperor was strong, so when the mobilisation took place the populations obeyed the drafts and marched." As the war went on it became harder to get a true picture. "There was press censorship. Austria was very strong — much stronger than Germany, in fact — in censoring information and presenting the events of the war in the best possible light. But we do know that at least initially there was loyalty to the empire, loyalty to the joint institutions of the monarchy, the Hungarian side and the Austrian side, and that generally speaking the people supported the decision to punish Serbia for its 'insolence', as they saw it."

The Austro-Hungarian leaders started out with relatively contained aims, but as the war expanded beyond the initial conflict with Serbia, as more and more nations joined the fight, their aims grew significantly. "The war aims initially were to defeat Serbia; punish it for its involvement in the assassination; reduce it by means of division among its other neighbours — principally

Bulgaria — to its size before the Balkan Wars; and reduce its access to the Adriatic," says Fried.

"Once the war escalated, Austria-Hungary's war aims escalated with it. The annexation of Montenegro was agreed; the annexation of parts of Wallachia, which was the southern part of Romania, and border territory in Romania; as well as the economic domination of Romania and Poland. That goal, hegemony of the entire Balkan Peninsula, is a rather large war aim, not a moderate one as has been portrayed in hindsight." And, he says, the extent to which that war aim compelled Austria-Hungary to fight on to its own destruction "is one of the most compelling [aspects] of its history".

In contrast to the response in Germany and Austria-Hungary, the prospect of war was not welcomed by the peoples of the Ottoman Empire. This once all-powerful empire, centred on Turkey, had begun its slow decline in the mid-16th century. In fact, according to US journalist and author Edwin Black, the British diplomat Sir Thomas Roe described it as "irrevocably sick" as far back as 1621.

But it was in the 19th century that this assessment really took off. In early 1853, British envoy Sir George Hamilton Seymour described in a dispatch to London a conversation he'd had with Russia's Nicholas I in which the Tsar described the Ottoman Empire as "a sick man … a very sick man". Despite attempts to shore the empire up from within, Leon Trotsky, who was based in Vienna as a war correspondent during the First and Second Balkan Wars, described how variations of the phrase — "the sick man of the Bosporus", "the sick man of the East" and, most famously, "the sick man of Europe" — took hold in the years following Seymour's dispatches. The First Balkan War, which took place between 1912 and 1913, was a successful attempt by the Balkan League states to capitalise on this perceived weakness.

Professor Mesut Uyar, whose books include the co-authored *A Military History of the Turks: From Osman to Ataturk*, notes that the outcome of that war — which saw the Ottoman Empire lose all its European land holdings — had a profound psychological effect. "The Ottoman leaderships and the Ottoman public could not understand how a big empire failed to defend its European territory against these small, small states." As well as the deep soul-searching that followed, "the Ottoman military somehow had to reorganise, re-equip, and try to create its army once again". There was, he says, widespread agreement at all levels, including the very top of the hierarchy, "that the Ottomans must stay away from any conflict at least three or four years."

Of course, in the end that didn't happen, and Uyar says that when Ottoman leaders declared they were mobilising at the beginning of August 1914, "people generally obeyed the mobilisation orders", but there were none of the "outbursts of happiness or joy or celebration that you see in London, in Berlin, in Vienna".

Austria-Hungary and the Ottoman Empire, each allied with Germany, formed a good working relationship with one another, says Marvin Fried, "on the basis that the enemy of my enemy is my friend". While the Austro-Hungarian relationship with the Turks wasn't as deep as Germany's, it was nonetheless "very positive". It was greatly helped by the fact that the pair had what Fried describes as "a common secret enemy" in the form of Bulgaria, which was intent on expanding its control within the Balkans: "The Austro-Hungarians and the Turks co-operated to keep Bulgaria in check and prevent it from becoming the next big south Slav 'mini great power' of the Balkans, which was the reason Austria-Hungary went to war with Serbia in the first place."

Germany exerted control over both its partners, but the degree of control differed. "Contrary to the Ottoman model, where you had German generals in charge, the Austro-Hungarians were very independent and maintained and insisted on that independence for as long as they could," says Fried. However, this didn't prevent the German generals from regarding "all fronts other than the Western Front and their own Eastern Front as side-shows".

Early in the war Germany saw a chance to use one of the Islamic world's central controlling mechanisms to its advantage via its connection with the Ottomans. The Caliphate can be thought of as a kind of Muslim equivalent to the Catholic concept of papacy; it exerts spiritual leadership over all the members of the religion no matter what their national allegiance. For six centuries caliphs had held authority over the Muslims of Spain, North Africa and the Middle East. Then in the 13th century the Mongols sacked Baghdad, effectively ending the Caliphate.

Over the following centuries various rulers, including Ottoman sultans, had declared themselves caliphs, but as their empire came under serious pressure the Ottomans pushed this claim harder.

Then, in November 1914, under the mantle of the Caliphate, Ottoman sultan Mehmen V declared a holy war, or *jihad*, against the members of the Entente — Britain, France and Russia — urging Muslims everywhere to rise up against them.

But, says Uyar, this declaration originated in Germany. "It was not designed in Istanbul, it was designed in Berlin," he explains. "Wilhelm II really believed in the power of Islam binding all Muslims all around the world. At that time the British Empire had millions of Muslims and the French colonial empire had millions of Muslims, especially in northern Africa. So the Germans believed that if the Ottoman Sultan, the Caliph of Islam, declared *jihad* against the French and the British it would create big problems, big rebellions. They were dreaming of a kind of wildfire, affecting whole areas from northern Africa to India."

Not only did that fail to happen, but the abolition of the Ottoman Empire that resulted from the Central Powers' loss in World War I also brought an end to both the Sultanate and the Caliphate.

With neither the Ottoman nor Austro-Hungarian Empires surviving, Germany was the focus for blame in the years following the war; at least, it was the focus outside Germany. Gerhard Hirschfeld says that up to the 1960s German historians were convinced that "nothing could be gained by looking into the question of guilt and responsibility further; they stuck to the old interpretation used during the Weimar period". Then in the 1960s, the work of historian Fritz Fischer ignited debate within Germany.

But even Fischer's work on World War I was seen in the light of the horrors of World War II. "For a long time, the Second World War overshadowed all events and the consequences of the First World War," says Hirschfeld. It is only recent analysis, he says, that allows us to see the First World War in a rather different light from the one in which our forefathers and previous generations saw it.

German Chancellor Angela Merkel referred to this when she opened the exhibition "The First World War: 1914–1918" at the German Historical Museum in Berlin in May 2014. "There was a lot of hesitance to talk about World War I, in part because of the guilt questions. By contrast, the guilt question for World War II was very clear," she said in a discussion with students at the event.

According to some commentators there is still too much hesitancy; they have criticised the German government's approach to centenary commemorations. While countries including France, Britain and Australia have planned major events to remember important moments and battles throughout the war, Germany's approach has been much more low-key.

German-born, British-based Dr Annika Mombauer is one who thinks the 100th anniversary should have been handled differently in Germany. She says that the sensitivities that still surround the war, particularly its causes, make finding the right tone difficult, but that doesn't mean the centenary should be ignored.

"I think it's actually really shocking that there is no attempt by the German government to commemorate a war that cost so many lives and led to such tragedy in Germany," she has said. "What you get is local initiatives commemorating the war in the Rhineland or the war in Bavaria or whatever it might be, because there is clearly a need to remember that war, but from the German government there's nothing."

Dr Claudia Sternberg, Senior Lecturer in Cultural Studies and a member of the Legacies of War Centenary project at the University of Leeds, was in Berlin at the German Historical Museum in 2014 when Chancellor

Merkel opened the World War I exhibition. She disagrees with the idea that Germany is doing "nothing" for the centenary. "If you are looking only at the central government and you expect some sort of agenda being imposed or public ceremonies, I don't think that's the way the Germans will want to remember or commemorate the First World War," she says. "It's also important to note that Germany is decentralised. You have state governments who do their own thing ... There are very, very many larger and smaller projects all around the country; there is much on the media — television drama, debates, and lots of news coverage; and many collaborations with other countries."

Sternberg agrees, though, that the Great War is "quite a distant memory" for most Germans: "There's not as much in-depth knowledge in the population at large. You would find a lot more knowledge around the Second World War and particularly the Holocaust, and how it came to be." The centenary years are, she says, a chance to fill in the gaps. But even those who may not have all the details at hand can appreciate the point Merkel made at the museum when she said Europe's unification was "the true lesson" of her country's history. It's striking,

Sternberg says, how much importance is placed on the unity of Europe in the German commemorations. The country has had "seventy years of peace, not war, and I think there's a genuine appreciation of this".

8

GOD AND COUNTRY

Did religion lead us into the conflict?

*... the stern hand of fate has scourged us to an elevation
where we can see the great everlasting things which
matter for a nation — the great peaks we had
forgotten, of Honour, Duty, Patriotism and, clad
in glittering white, the great pinnacle of Sacrifice
pointing like a rugged finger to Heaven.*

— David Lloyd George, Chancellor of the Exchequer,
September 1914

For some historians, including Philip Jenkins, there is
no question about the importance of the influence of
religion on World War I. Professor Jenkins, author of *The
Great and Holy War: How World War I Became a Religious
Crusade*, says that the years leading up to 1914 were a

time of strong religious belief in many countries including Russia — something that is often forgotten because of the Russian Revolution in 1917.

Not only was Russia sometimes known as "a church with a state" as opposed to the other way around, but the Russian people also held "messianic, millenarian ideas. They still read these ancient prophesies about how an emperor was to rise who would liberate the Middle East and destroy the Turks and the Muslims. Very responsible Russian intellectuals took those ideas seriously and that shaped how they acted in the years up to 1914. That messianic ideal was there very strongly."

In fact, Jenkins says Russia was experiencing a full-scale religious revival reaching deep into the hearts of intellectuals, of thinkers, of city dwellers. "For the first time ever you had Orthodox preachers who were reaching ordinary workers in the cities and the factories. That seems incredible when you look at what's going to happen in 1917, but the fact of modernity does not clash with a religious revival." Instead, "mystical, esoteric, occult ideas were very widespread, particularly among artists and intellectuals, and they too were expecting an apocalypse within the near future".

In Germany, too, there was religious fervour, but expression of belief was very different there to the elaborate rituals of the Russian Orthodox Church; in Germany it was the austere Lutheran branch of Protestantism that predominated.

"Germany was a very new nation in 1914. It was united in 1871 and many German intellectuals saw that literally as a miraculous event," Jenkins explains. Four decades post-unification they believed that Germany had a divine destiny to shape Europe's future. This belief was explicitly articulated by Lutheran religious leaders. As war loomed, pastors and preachers and bishops spoke in "the language of a new Pentecost: Germany was undergoing a transfiguration and it would 'remodel Europe in its own guise as the Kingdom of God'."

Thus, says Jenkins, in the lead-up to the war, both Russia and Germany were operating on the belief that they have been given a divine mission. Unfortunately for the world, "Europe didn't really have room for two messianic nations creating the Kingdom of God".

Religion was also exerting a strong influence elsewhere, including in countries such as France. Although it was officially "very secular", Jenkins says, "The soldiers and the ordinary people were absolutely convinced that they were marching forward in a crusade — literally — against Lutheran Protestant Germany; what they called 'black Luther's dark hordes'."

In Britain, David Lloyd George, who in 1914 was chancellor of the exchequer (and in 1916 would become prime minister), was also framing his support for the war in terms of a higher calling. "You read his rhetoric, with the language he uses about sacrifice and blood and destiny," says Jenkins. "It's very religious language. In *Mein Kampf,* Hitler wrote he regarded David Lloyd George as the greatest orator who'd ever lived and he modelled himself on him."

The result of all this was that "as they went into 1914, a great many people around the world already held ideas of imminent apocalypse, of holy war, of religious conflict. It was something they were used to, together with ideas of redemptive sacrifice, shedding your blood for the nation. Governments did not have to work hard to build on this … A lot of the bloodiest, most war-like rhetoric is actually coming from mainstream churches and the states just have to follow along."

Dr Joseph Loconte, author of the forthcoming *A Hobbit, a Wardrobe and a Great War: How C.S. Lewis and*

J.R.R. Tolkien Rediscovered Faith, Friendship and Heroism in the Cataclysm of 1914–18, concurs. "That rhetoric of blessing the patriotic aims, the military aims of your country, and enmeshing it in religious language happened really across the board. Virtually all sides were involved in that kind of religious rhetoric."

There were dissenters to this martial enthusiasm, religious figures who spoke out strongly against going to war. But, says Jenkins, "it's very surprising how marginalised those anti-war voices were". In fact when Pope Pius X died on 20 August 1914, just weeks after the conflict had begun, the Archbishop of Sydney, Michael Kelly, said, "The world is having war because it gave up Christianity and the one man who could have made peace among the nations died of a broken heart."

Pius's successor, Pope Benedict XV, fared no better in terms of influencing the combatants to lay down their arms. Jenkins says Benedict "spoke about the horror of Christians killing Christians. He gave out very plausible, sensible plans for a workable peace and for European disarmament. And around the world all the Catholic countries and Catholic powers pretty much universally ignored him."

Joseph Loconte agrees that religious language was used to promote the war but he argues that Christianity at the time had taken on "a kind of political function": the social gospel movement, which applied Christian ethics to social problems, was booming not only in the United States but also in Great Britain. He warns against "confusing that kind of Christian nationalism with a genuine, authentic religious piety" and says a new idea was taking hold. "As the historic Christian faith is weakening and — to some degree in the United States but particularly in Europe — as the fundamental doctrines of heaven and hell and judgment and sin and redemption are fading away, you need a replacement. And the replacement becomes the nation state; it becomes the notion of progress itself."

"Progress" justified a great many things, including the sacrifice of lives. "One of the most common and popular and deeply rooted ideas by the end of the 19th and the early 20th century is that Western civilisation is on an upward trend," Loconte says. "Progress is the watchword to such a degree that even war itself could be seen as a progressive thing, as a redemptive thing, as something that would bring about an improvement in the human condition and in human societies ... So, many religious leaders, particularly the more religiously liberal leaders, got caught up in the notion of progress in a way that's deeply troubling."

Ultimately, he says, the war was "a political conflict. It was about power. It was about geography. It was about the domination of resources." But "because Europe was still nominally Christian at that point and because of the close relationship of Church and state throughout the European continent, it couldn't help but to some degree take on the feel of a holy crusade".

British journalist Peter Hitchens is the author of a number of books including *The Rage Against God*, which chronicles his own shift from atheism to Christianity and counters the views expressed in his (now late) brother Christopher's book *God Is Not Great*. He agrees that the support shown for the war by various churches including the Church of England, to which he belongs, seriously harmed their reputations and credibility. "Initially, in the first months of war, the Church was extremely, almost shockingly, enthusiastic about the war, and it associated in people's minds the Church hierarchy with the political hierarchy, with all the other frock-coated, white-haired old geezers who were saying, 'This war is one in which we must all — or rather *you* must all — go off and risk your lives because the cause is great'."

Specifically, Hitchens says, it was characterised as "a great war for civilisation" ("those words were actually inscribed on the medals issued to those who served in the war at the end") and "the war to end all wars". "That sustained it as a crusade even after the horrible carnage became known, when people realised the immense butcher's bill we'd paid for it; that sustained it until 1939 when it became quite clear that it hadn't ended war at all."

Rather than "a war between good and bad", he says, World War I "started as an old-fashioned land grab". However, the conflict was given a very particular spin by the leaders of the day. "One must remember that it was, perhaps, the first democratic war. On the side of the Allies the countries involved — you have to leave out Russia in this calculation — France and Britain and later the United States and of course the Anzac contribution as well, these were democracies. And as Winston Churchill said prophetically in 1901, the wars of democracies will be much more savage than the wars of kings."

Hitchens says that Churchill "understood that to arouse a democracy against an enemy you're going to have to tell the people that this is a crusade, that this is a sacred war. Having done that, you can't then compromise. You have to fight to the end because you've declared your enemy to be so evil that a compromise would itself be evil ... undoubtedly this was the reason why many attempts to reach a negotiated peace failed, because the democratic leaders of the Allied countries simply couldn't find any way of selling such a beast to the population, whom they'd told, 'We're engaging in a crusade.' This belief that it was a holy war was very, very widespread and very powerful in changing its course."

Any discussion of religious and spiritual motivations for World War I inevitably circles around to the influence of Prussian-German philosopher and cultural critic Friedrich Nietzsche ... despite the fact that he died 14 years before it began.

Nietzsche, surely one of history's most misunderstood and misquoted figures, famously wrote, "God is dead." But the context of this claim is too often omitted. He was expounding the view that after thousands of years in which belief in God supplied purpose and moral guidance, 19th-century life had brought a decline in faith and a rise in atheism that would lead to chaos and nihilism.

Nietzsche died in 1900, leaving his work as a kind of Rorschach test for those who came later. People of every political and philosophical stripe have taken him up over the years, cherry-picking his work for the parts that have seemed to support their own ideas. By far the most famous misappropriation was that of the Nazis a generation after his death. This association, which irrevocably tainted his name, was largely due to Nietzsche's anti-Semitic, pro-Hitler sister Elisabeth, his literary executor.

The Nazi association cemented the idea that Nietzsche was an aggressive warmonger, but the idea had risen even before that. This was partly to the fact that Nietzsche's book *Thus Spoke Zarathustra* was issued to some German frontline soldiers during World War I, and partly because of the approving way feted German soldier Ernst Jünger quoted Nietzsche in his enthusiastic war memoir, *Storm of Steel*. But historian Dr Hugo Drochon, who specialises in Nietzsche and modern European political ideas, says this image of the philosopher does him a grave disservice. "In fact I think the war would have been the manifestations of his deepest fears. One way of trying to think about what his reaction would have been is to look at the reactions he had to the Franco-Prussian War, which he experienced as a medical orderly. At first he was very enthusiastic about it, but he quickly came to realise that it ended up representing all the things that he would come to label as herd morality. Namely, it was a move toward nationalism, philistinism, mediocrity, democracy: all the things that he came to hate."

William Altman — whose book *Friedrich Wilhelm Nietzsche: The Philosopher of the Second Reich* examines Nietzsche's influence on Germany between unification and the end of World War I — agrees. "Nietzsche wrote a great deal about being a good European. The elite of all nations, a trans-national elite, was something that he had in mind, rather than a German elite. German nationalism nauseated him, and I think nationalism generally did."

In the pre-war years Nietzsche's ideas were used to shore up both the extreme right and the extreme left in Europe and the US, says Drochon. "But what happened with the outbreak of the war was an attempt at appropriation by the German authorities of Nietzsche. We must remember the other two books that were given to the soldiers along with *Thus Spoke Zarathustra* were the New Testament and Goethe's *Faust*." The intended message was "This is German culture; it's what we're fighting for."

But in "the din of war" the specificity of this message was lost and Nietzsche became inextricably linked in many people's minds with German martial culture.

Drochon adds, "It's true that the martial language you get in *Thus Spoke Zarathustra* may have appealed to the soldiers at the front," even though "it's rarely a question of physical warfare; it's a lot of intellectual warfare. It's about overcoming one's self".

Altman has a slightly different take. "I don't think I would style it as strictly intellectual warfare. I think that there's a lot of talking about death and dying and fighting and being ready to die." For him the appeal of Nietzsche's world-view to young German soldiers in the war's later years lay in what they had to endure. "Germany found herself fighting a two-front war, and as the supplies began to run short and as the army began to starve, the kind of privation that the German soldiers suffered made them very ripe for Nietzsche." Specifically, Altman says, the "tragic pessimism" running through his writing spoke to them. The ones to whom it spoke most strongly were the elite troops, including Jünger, who were formed into specialist assault units; these "handpicked, culled, excellent soldiers creamed off the top of the German army, who were reckless and ready to fight" became "Nietzsche's disciples".

"A lot of people went into the war with very high ideals as to what was going to happen: 'the war is going to be over very soon'; or 'we're going to achieve all our aims'; or 'we're here to defend our national honour and culture'," says Drochon. "Very, very high expectations, which were dashed relatively quickly." Authority came under scrutiny and Christianity was among the foundational beliefs thrown into question, which gave much of Nietzsche's subject matter, such as "what you do after the death of God, how do you try to have some kind of values", an urgent new appeal.

But spiritualism and religion in the war weren't only about sweeping statements and the justification of national positions. For some of those doing the fighting they had a very personal resonance. One example was the phenomenon of unearthly manifestations reported by those on both sides.

To understand this we need to shake off our modern perceptions, says Philip Jenkins. In this day and age might think of angels as something found on greeting cards, but for many of those on the frontlines they were real and powerful. "In Catholic and Orthodox tradition especially, angels feature in the book of Revelation, they fight the devil in the last times, and visions of angels are an important part of the apocalyptic vision."

Perhaps the best-known story of supernatural manifestation is that of the "Angel of Mons". The story took place during the retreat by heavily outnumbered British troops at Mons, Belgium, in August 1914. A heavenly presence, often said to be St George, supposedly appeared before the desperate Tommys, frightening the Germans so much they halted their advance, which saved the British from certain devastation.

The tale, which came to be widely believed, is thought to have originated as a short story by Arthur Machen called "The Bowmen", set during the Mons retreat and published in London's *Evening News* the month after the battle. In Machen's story, long-dead bowmen are summoned by St George and fire off their phantom weapons to great effect.

By 1915, retellings of this angelic intervention as fact were popping up throughout Britain in sermons, magazines and books about the war. Machen wasn't backwards in claiming credit for inventing the story, but others, including the devoutly Christian journalist Harold Begbie, put huge effort into trying to prove that "eyewitness accounts" of this and other angelic appearances pre-dated Machen's work. Begbie probably didn't need to try so hard: many people were eager to believe that angels did exist and intervened at various places, not just Mons. "The Russians have their angelic visions. The French have their stories of dead soldiers rising to fight at the front," says Jenkins.

The new art form of cinema also promoted otherworldly ideas, he says. "The greatest film of the war is D.W. Griffith's *Intolerance* in 1916, which ends with a vision of angels appearing over the Western Front and ushering in the last judgment and the end of the world."

And then there were the repeated visions of the Virgin Mary claimed by a 10-year-old Portuguese girl and two of her cousins at Fatima in 1917. The girl, Lucia dos Santos, claimed Mary had said to her, "Russia will spread its errors throughout the world, raising up wars and persecutions of the Church. The good will be martyred, the Holy Father will have much to suffer, and various nations will be annihilated." This vision, coming, says Jenkins, "at one of the most dangerous, desperate moments of the war, is pretty much universally believed across the Catholic world".

It wasn't only the men in the trenches who had spiritual beliefs, says Jenkins. Both sides had generals who were "extremely religious, though not necessarily in orthodox ways. With the great battles on the Western Front in 1918, on both the German and the British sides you have generals who are deep into mystical and esoteric movements. General Ludendorff is a Neopagan. On the other side, the great general who invents modern armoured warfare is J.F.C. Fuller, who's a disciple of the great mystical occult leader Aleister Crowley. So, in one sense, a magician is fighting a magician. Spiritualist ideas, theosophical ideas are everywhere. In some ways it's harder to find somebody who isn't following these ideas than people who are."

But the war and its aftermath wrought huge changes on the world's major religions, some of which are still playing out today. It was, says Jenkins, a catastrophic period for Christianity. "Today we think of Protestant and Catholic. Back in 1914 there was Protestant, Catholic and Orthodox. But the Orthodox world was extremely hard hit. The Russian Revolution launched one of the greatest religious persecutions in Christian history. Christianity was also destroyed across large parts of the Middle East. Armenian and Syrian communities that had been Christian since apostolic times were massacred in the millions."

In addition, he says, "There was also a great intellectual change, which is that after 1918 it's very hard to believe in the traditional idea of Christendom, of the Church and the state working side by side. Theologians like Karl Barth spent many decades trying to devise a new basis on which Christianity can proceed, and in some ways, theologians are still battling with this idea."

For Peter Hitchens, the damage was caused by religious and political leaders' use of Christian tenets to support the war: "One of the things which has to be at the very heart of the Christian religion is that if violence is to be done at all, it has to be done for justice. If you portray something as just which isn't and you do that in the name of faith, then it has to rebound onto the faith that's being used to do so, doesn't it?"

The war also fundamentally changed Judaism, says Jenkins. "When the war starts, Jews in various countries — Germany, Russia, Britain, France — become very committed to their particular country because they hope that national activity, that service, will earn them full assimilation. In some cases, that works. But in Germany especially, as the war goes bad in 1916, the Jews become scapegoats. And that is the point at which many Jews who previously had rejected Zionism start thinking, 'We had better have a refuge for when really serious dangers happen in Europe.'"

Jenkins argues that the other major force in play here was "very messianic- and apocalyptic-inclined Christian politicians in Europe who were prepared to see the Jews' return to Palestine as part of the apocalyptic scheme. It's in 1917 that the British issue the Balfour Declaration, which is the charter for the establishment of the modern state of Israel. So the two greatest developments in Jewish history in the 20th century, the Holocaust and the establishment of the state of Israel, both have their roots not just in the First World War but in 1917."

Loconte agrees that "the stirrings of anti-Semitism in Germany is one of the consequences of the First World War. Germans are looking for a scapegoat in part to explain their betrayal at the Treaty of Versailles and they will find that scapegoat in the Jewish people. So we're set up for the Holocaust in the fires of the First World War."

Islam was also profoundly affected. The war, of course, brought the end of the Islamic Ottoman Empire, and more specifically, observes Jenkins, "the end of the Caliphate. We are only really beginning to see how important that was. All around the world, for the first time in centuries, it galvanises Muslims to joint political action. Jihad warfare and rebellions rage across North Africa and Asia all the way from 1918 into the late 1920s; there are probably 20 or 30 separate guerrilla wars in progress. It's at that point, for example, that because of the Caliphate issue Indian Muslims developed the idea of an independent state: the seeds of the later partition of India. The war changed everything for the Muslims as well as for Jews and Christians." (For more on the Caliphate see Chapter 7.)

Loconte says, "Dr Jenkins has done us a service in reminding us how Islam was so profoundly affected by the break-up of the Ottoman Empire and then the revulsion against a colonial rule. We're dealing with the consequence of that now — the conflict playing out in Iraq, for example. These are social and spiritual consequences of the First World War that we're living with 100 years later."

9

OTHER VOICES, OTHER BATTLES

Who were the forgotten millions who also served?

Please compile for war census purposes the following
information regarding Aborigines and half-castes
in your district … List of civilised male Aborigines
between 18–45 years …

— John William Bleakley, Queensland's Chief
Protector of Aborigines, 1915

Of the scores, maybe hundreds, of photographs you've seen from World War I, how many showed soldiers wearing turbans? Or Chinese tank mechanics? Or African bearers? Millions of people who didn't have white skin participated in the war — willingly or otherwise, in combat or in support roles — yet their contributions have been largely forgotten until now.

When the war broke out, imperial interests controlled much of the planet. The Ottoman Empire was shrinking, but Britain, France, Russia and Germany between them ruled over two-fifths of the world's population — around 700 million people. They had no hesitation in drawing on these people to satisfy their war needs.

Britain alone called upon the services of almost 2.5 million men from its Dominions, 1.4 million of them Indian volunteers. Around one million of these men would see overseas service. No wonder *The Times* of London declared, "The Indian Empire has overwhelmed the British by the completeness and unanimity of its enthusiastic aid."

It wasn't really unanimous, though. While a number of key figures in India, including Mohandas K. Gandhi, believed that supporting Britain's war aims would be a stepping stone to more independence — Home Rule — others disagreed. One doubter was senior Congress Party and Muslim League member Mohammad Ali Jinnah. As late as 1918 Gandhi was still trying to convince him to change his mind, writing him a letter in which he paraphrased the Bible: "I do wish you would make an emphatic declaration regarding recruitment ... 'Seek ye first the recruiting office and everything will be added unto you.'"

Dr Gajendra Singh is the author of *The Testimonies of Indian Soldiers and the Two World Wars*. He says that just over half of all the Indian Army soldiers recruited came from a single province, the Punjab in the northwest. This was no coincidence. British military recruiters had firmly entrenched racial theories: "quite detailed ethnographies about where one can find the best recruits and who is fit for recruitment, who's fit for enlistment."

The theories were codified in handbooks which detailed "everything from castes, to folk memories, to nasal measurements", designed to identify "the right kind of recruit". Punjabis were favoured because of climatic theories. The idea was, says Singh, "Indians may have been white once, but the warm climate had somehow enervated their race". Following this theory, recruiters believed it was in places such as the Punjab, with its cold winter, that "one could find remnants of the most martial of all Indians".

For all the emphasis on recruitment documentation, the reality in what was then a heavily rural country with low literacy rates was that identification documents for the recruits themselves were often completely absent, allowing underage boys to slip through. "I found evidence of soldiers as young as 14 enlisting," says Singh. "They were not actually allowed to enlist that young, 16 was the age. But in India, where there was no real proper way of judging someone's age, a young boy who was quite large, who had the requisite chest measurements, could quite easily enlist."

As to why Indian men and boys would want to sign up, Singh says it was a matter of both immediate survival and longer-term hopes. Recruits tended to come from "areas suffering from high levels of rural indebtedness and high levels of rural landlessness". For these Indians there was no real prospect of paid employment other than joining the army. Many were also drawn by the belief that having served, they would be able to secure government jobs.

Singh was able to conduct his research by reading the thousands of letters written by or for Indian soldiers during the war. They survive thanks to a security measure introduced by British leaders suspicious of the rebellious tendencies of their troops. When Indian soldiers began disembarking in Marseilles at the end of September 1914, the Indian Army and the British military establishment found seditious, revolutionary and nationalist literature. Singh says the material came from "a small group of Indian nationalists who were operating in France at the time". A small group it might have been, but the reaction to this discovery was a very large one. A Censor of Indian Mails was established and what Singh calls a "massive corpus of letters" was collected, transcribed and translated, leaving an extraordinary record for historians to study.

The majority of Indian soldiers served only a year in France before being moved elsewhere (in 1915 the infantry divisions were sent to Palestine, Mesopotamia and Gallipoli in the racially based belief that they were better suited to warm-weather fighting). But that year was long enough for fraternisation between Indian soldiers and local women, which caused great concern to authorities in both France and Britain. For those who believed in "racial purity", the thought of children who might result from this mingling was highly disturbing.

"The dangers of what in France was called the métis or the mixed-race child, was a real panic," says Singh.

"You start having petitions being made to the French government by French women who want to marry Indian military personnel, something that was forbidden in the Indian Army, and this becomes a problem." In due course the Indian Army changed its rules to allow its soldiers to marry French women — but only certain soldiers: Muslims. "The idea is that if you are an Indian Muslim you cannot control your lascivious sexual urges," says Singh. "If you are a Sikh or Hindu, you somehow can. It's very odd and very convoluted."

There was a very different response in Britain, where three hospitals were set up in or around Brighton for wounded Indian troops. Care was put into planning so that different religious groups had their food prepared in separate kitchens, and prayer rooms were provided. At first the convalescing soldiers were a very welcome presence. The local *Herald* published a supplement on them. King George V came to visit and made the rounds. The Indian men were asked to tea by locals or taken for visits to the seaside.

Unsurprisingly, says Singh, relationships soon began to develop between the patients and the young women of the area. As in France, authorities saw this as a significant problem. "Colonel Bruce Seaton is running the biggest hospital in Brighton, the Kitchener Indian Hospital, and the solution he adopts is to forbid any interaction between Indian wounded and the people of Brighton." Amongst other measures, barbed wire was installed around the hospital precincts to prevent anyone from slipping out. The punishments, says Singh, were draconian. Men who were caught trying to get into the town were flogged.

This didn't just happen to convalescents, he says: "Indian soldiers in the First World War were routinely flogged." It was not a punishment meted out to the British soldiers fighting alongside them. "This unique punishment, this unique treatment, leads to Indian soldiers in their letters questioning their identities, questioning their reasons for fighting, in quite profound ways."

Despite often harsh treatment during the war, the Indian soldiers were collectively lionised afterwards, credited with extraordinary courage during battle. But Singh says this, too, is a racially motivated simplification that needs to be discarded in favour of the more nuanced truth. "The reality is that those who fought in the war, whether they were Indian, or Australian or British, were as inadequate, as anxious, as insecure as we are today. If one looks at war testimonies by Indian soldiers, by French soldiers, by British soldiers, we see the same levels of fear, of panic, of just being unable to comprehend this nightmare scenario that they are in."

Indian soldiers were among the many nationalities that fought in Africa — a theatre that is almost completely ignored in many discussions of World War I.

As the war began, France and Britain controlled huge swathes of the continent, but Germany, Belgium, Portugal, Italy and Spain all had African colonies too. The exact numbers of black Africans who fought alongside the Europeans, Indians and white South Africans will never be known, but historian Dr Paul Mulvey has estimated that at least 80,000 were combatants for one side or the other, of whom 10,000 died, and up to two million more Africans were used as labour.

Sir Hew Strachan, author of books including *The First World War In Africa*, explains that for every ordinary soldier deployed, two or three men were needed to carry baggage; even more for officers. "This was a war that was really carried on men's backs over enormous distances," he says, noting that while there were some railways in sub-Saharan Africa before 1914, they did not generally travel in the directions in which the armies were moving. "That meant black labour was conscripted — conscripted is probably a euphemism in some cases — to carry not just food, but ammunition."

It became a self-perpetuating problem: the greater the distance to be covered and the longer the line of people marching, the more food that would need to be brought along, which meant more carriers, which meant more food to feed them. "So the exponential effects of a march of, let's say, 100 miles compared to a march of 10 miles is quite extraordinary in the demand it generates for labour," says Strachan.

This demand should, in theory, have benefited the Africans who supplied the labour, says Strachan. There was competition between white settlers, who needed labour on their land to continue the pre-1914 pattern of agricultural productivity, and the demand for labour for military columns. This should have led to a pricing war, but the colonial authorities were not about to allow that to happen. Rather than allow increased demand to increase wages, they introduced conscription. A very specific sort of conscription.

"Conscription describes a legal process, which may be inappropriate in this context," Strachan says. "What would happen much more routinely is that the colonial power would go to a local chief and say, 'I need 20 men.' And the colonial chief would provide the men, who'd probably be the 20 he didn't want in the community any longer — the trouble-makers or people that were undesirable from his point of view."

It wasn't just being compelled to serve that affected the lives of native Africans. Serving as labour for these travelling armies also produced significant geographic dislocation. "What it does — and I think we often forget this — is take Africans out of their own area," says Strachan. "So you are creating enormous mobility in this population, and enormous disruption. Very often whole families are occupied in this business of carrying: if a man is carrying, his wife and children would come too, perhaps in order to feed him and support him. And very often all of them will succumb to disease because, despite the European assumption that they will be resistant, they are being exposed to new infections, new sources of disease and new diets as they move into an unfamiliar part of the continent."

Paul Mulvey has said that perhaps 10 per cent of all the conscripted Africans died. There are no concrete figures, just guestimates based on the recorded demand for additional manpower as the war progresses. The causes of the casualties were very different to those elsewhere, especially on the Western Front. In sub-Saharan Africa sickness was the big problem for all the armies, and mortality rates were high. "Disease was the killer, not battle," says Strachan.

It's not just firm figures that are lacking. We know very little about the overall experience of these Africans, including how they were treated by the forces they were serving. In part, says Strachan, that's because they came from oral cultures, not written ones. "And even at the oral level, by the time historians were awoken to their experience it was the 1970s and 1980s. There were very few survivors to speak to."

It's also because anything gleaned from records kept by the colonial officers themselves needs to be treated with caution. "Remember, after the war the whole imperial enterprise is under challenge," says Strachan. "Germany's lost its colonies. Britain is confronting the challenge of the United States, with its queries about British imperialism. And although the British Empire after 1918 is at its greatest ever extent, it is in that situation largely thanks to mandates." Mandates were the authorisations handed out by the League of Nations which gave the war's victors control over colonial territories previously held by Germany or the Ottoman Empire. Given that the each of the Allies had said annexing more territory was not a motivation to enter the war, the mandates were seen as temporary arrangements — some more temporary than others.

The upshot, Strachan says, was that Germany, Britain and France now had to justify their positions as colonial powers. "And that means they want to put the best face on how they treat the native population. So they are not going to say a great deal on paper about brutality and the way in which they handled these people. They are going to present themselves as the inspired leaders of very loyal Africans. And broadly speaking, that is how it is presented in the memoir literature in the 1920s."

Despite the fact that this part of the war had involved millions of people, it remained more or less forgotten for decades. That situation has improved, but enormous gaps still remain. Strachan and other latter-day historians are working to try to develop a more complete picture. The Africans who were caught up in the war, he says, "deserve to be recognised and appreciated. They are much more a part of the story."

The gap in our knowledge about the war in Africa is one thing, but given how closely detailed the Western Front has been, it is nothing less than astonishing to learn that 140,000 Chinese ended up serving there.

Professor Xu Guoqi, author of *Strangers on the Western Front: Chinese Workers in the Great War*, explains that the seeds of this participation were sown when Japan defeated China in the Sino-Japanese War at the end of the previous century. "When the European war broke out, China was in the middle of a transformation. In 1895, when China was invaded by the Japanese, the Chinese had started to search for a new national identity, a new direction. From that moment on, the Chinese were trying to join the world. So when Germany launched the First World War the Chinese had quite mixed feelings about the news. *Weiji* is the Chinese term, *wei* meaning danger and *ji* an opportunity."

The danger, he says, was that with the major powers otherwise occupied, the Japanese might attempt to turn China into a dependent state. The opportunity was in the expectation that the war would destroy the existing world order, allowing China to take its place at the global table. Attempting to seize this opportunity, China tried to join the Entente Allies when war broke out in the European summer of 1914. Great Britain, however, rejected the Chinese offer.

Things went very differently for the Japanese, British allies since 1902. They were quick off the mark, declaring war on Germany on 23 August, less than three weeks after Britain. This gave legitimacy to their plan to capture Germany's largest overseas naval base, which happened to be Tsingtao (Qingdao) on China's Shandong Peninsula. With the help of two British battalions, 60,000 Japanese troops blockaded the base, forcing a German surrender on 7 November. But in doing so, the Japanese had violated Chinese neutrality. It was the thin end of the wedge. Two months later, in January 1915, Japan presented its "21 Demands" to China, including many territorial annexations, most of which the weakened country was forced to accept.

China then tried again to join the war and this time, says Xu, Great Britain, France and Russia welcomed it. There was, however, a problem. Japan strongly opposed the move. The Chinese responded with what Xu describes as a creative strategy: sending workers to Europe in the place of soldiers. Many did not survive the journey, thanks to German submarine attacks — at least 700 were killed on just one of the torpedoed ships. But the first group of Chinese workers arrived in France in early 1916.

In all, around 140,000 would serve, of whom the British recruited around 100,000. Xu says they almost all worked near the front, digging trenches, loading and unloading ammunition and repairing roads. But around 1,500 became dedicated tank repairers. "In the beginning the British soldiers tried to prevent anybody from accessing the tanks, but they realised the Chinese were very skilled in this type of job. So eventually they commissioned three major companies of Chinese to work on the tanks. Even though the majority of the Chinese were often illiterate and less educated, and did not speak English or French, they were very skilled and very smart. I would argue they contributed enormously to the war effort of the Allies," he says.

For soldiers, the end of the war meant the end of the immediate threat to their lives. Not so the Chinese labourers. Their death rate actually climbed after the armistice because they were set to work filling in trenches, cleaning up the battlefields and doing other dangerous jobs. "They were having to handle live bombs and mines," says Xu. "Remember, they are workers, they were not trained to handle live ammunition. So, many Chinese actually died after the war when they got involved in the French national reconstruction."

Several of these Chinese workers received medals for their bravery in actions including extinguishing fires in ammunition stores at great personal risk, but their contribution was soon virtually forgotten. "The French government did not give them credit until the late 1990s," says Xu. "The British government still have not given them the credit they deserve. The Chinese government forgot them as well. Even today, the Chinese don't know very much about this extraordinary group of people who crossed the ocean to get involved in the so-called war for civilisation."

You might have thought that such an omission couldn't happen in Australia; that its extensive service records and documentation would mean that the contributions of everyone who served would be recognised. But that's not so for Indigenous servicemen. As with the African experience, this is something historians have tried to redress in recent years, yet much remains unknown, including exactly how many Indigenous Australians signed up. Estimates put the number at around 1,200.

Gary Oakley, Indigenous Liaison Officer at the Australian War Memorial, is one of those trying to shine a light on these untold stories. "Most Indigenous soldiers came back to Australia and went into community and disappeared. Silent heroes. They didn't draw attention to themselves. They didn't march on Anzac Day, so when people watched the battalions march past they did not see any black faces. It skewed, I think, the public's perception of the service of Indigenous Australians. It's really only now, and probably in the last five or ten years, that it's coming out. This is secret history that needs to be told."

When the war started the armed services were among the many Australian institutions that explicitly discriminated against Indigenous people, who were decades off gaining citizenship, had few rights under the law and, if they were paid wages, generally received a fraction of what a white person earned. The Defence Act specifically prohibited Aboriginal (and other Indigenous) men from serving. (The law would not be changed until 1949.) Indigenous Australians fronted up to enlistment centres only to be turned away at the door, although some who "didn't look Aboriginal" managed to get through.

But as the war dragged on, the moves to introduce conscription failed, and the overall numbers enlisting dropped, Australia's military commanders decided they could use Indigenous servicemen after all. In October 1917 a new Military Order was issued which declared, "Half-castes may be enlisted in the Australian Imperial Force provided that the examining Medical Officers are satisfied that one of the parents is of European origin." This highly subjective measure meant that some men applied two or three times before they were accepted, says Philippa Scarlett, author of *Aboriginal and Torres Strait Islander Volunteers for the AIF: The Indigenous Response to World War One.*

As to why Indigenous men wished to serve, Oakley says, "Patriotism might have been part of it. Also, there was the opportunity to be paid a wage — six shillings a day, which was good money, and you had the opportunity to send that back to your community or to your family." Some men who were still close to their traditional roots might have wanted to demonstrate their capabilities as warriors, he says. Others might have hoped "that when you came back to society, people may look upon you differently because you have served your nation".

Scarlett adds that "surprisingly, loyalty to king and country was a major factor for Indigenous war service. It comes out in a lot of the contemporary documents and letters, on the service records from the men themselves and their relatives."

If they made it past the enlistment process, Indigenous men found a very different environment to the one in which they lived day to day. For all the hardships of war, it was often a better one. "I always tell people that the Australian army was the first equal opportunity employer of Indigenous Australians," says Oakley. "In the Defence Force, you cannot have a prejudice. You have to rely on the man next to you in the trench. You can't have a problem with him, because he's going to have to watch your back. I found, looking through documentation, very few cases within the Defence Force of racism. I've come across a few, but it is very rare. Usually, when non-Indigenous Australians are talking about their Indigenous mates in the army, they talk about them in quite glowing terms."

This acceptance had to be earned, though; it wasn't a given. Indigenous men started out on the back foot.

"I think there were a number of levels where racism was experienced," says Scarlett. "There was the feeling that because they were Aboriginal, they wouldn't be good fighters. A man in Palestine said, 'We were very doubtful about whether we could rely on them and how they would perform. But after they had been in battle, they gained our respect.'"

And even when Indigenous soldiers had gained this respect and acceptance, she says, the pervasive views of the day shaped the way it was expressed by white soldiers. "I found they talk about them in glowing terms, but unfortunately being white was the measure of a man's worth." This led to "compliments" such as describing an Aboriginal man as "clear white inside" or saying of a comrade killed in France, "Although he was a half-Aboriginal he was a good fellow."

"Even the men who admired their fellow Aboriginal soldiers couldn't get past racism and the White Australia Policy that had really brainwashed all Australians," says Scarlett.

Indigenous soldiers were to be found in many different theatres of the war. "They served on Gallipoli. They served in France and Belgium. They served in Palestine and

Syria," says Oakley. "They served anywhere the Australian military put their feet on the ground." A number received decorations for gallantry. Private (Raymond) Charlie Runga was one. Fighting on the Western Front with the 6th Battalion, he was so severely wounded he spent six months recuperating. Just days after re-joining his unit he performed an extraordinary act near Herleville Wood for which he was awarded the Military Medal.

As his citation puts it, "When the left portion of his company came under exceptionally heavy machine gun fire from a wood in front, Pte Runga, taking charge of a small party, dashed to the wood and succeeded in capturing two hostile machine guns and their crew of 16 men. On another occasion he rushed forward alone over 70 yards of ground without cover and despite point-blank machine gun fire, succeeded in bombing the enemy from the communication trench … this latter feat was a heroic example of utter disregard for personal safety and the desire, at all costs, to worst the enemy, any of whom with one shot calmly aimed could have killed him." Philippa Scarlett says Runga's story shows that "in the heat of the battle, when the chips are down, it doesn't really matter what your colour is — it's the sort of man you are".

10

ENDGAME

How big a part did America and Russia play in Germany's defeat?

No statesman who has the least conception of his responsibility ought for a moment to permit himself to continue this tragical and appalling outpouring of blood and treasure unless he is sure beyond a peradventure that the objects of the vital sacrifice are part and parcel of the very life of Society ...

— Woodrow Wilson, US President,
8 January 1918

By the time the USA joined World War I in 1917 it had spent almost three years observing the raging conflict from afar. Its status was officially neutral, but the country and its people had been affected by the war right from the beginning.

At the outbreak of war in 1914 more than US$4 billion worth of railroad stocks and bonds was owned by non-Americans, three-quarters of it by British interests. These holdings were liquid assets, meaning they could be sold off very quickly for cash on the New York Stock Exchange and the sellers could demand banks exchange the cash for gold. If only the British owners took this option and even then only sold five per cent of their holdings, New York's banks would lose half their total gold reserves. Fearing such a result and the panicked run on banks it might provoke, the US government asked the New York Stock Exchange to close on 31 July 1914 and kept it closed for the next four and a half months.

This, explains Professor Michael Neiberg, author of *Dance of the Furies: Europe and the Outbreak of World War I*, was only one of the tremors felt in the US. America was already undergoing what he describes as a minor recession; the outbreak of war in Europe plunged the country into an economic crisis on par with the great economic crises of American history, including 1929. A bumper cotton crop combined with a major drop in the export demand for cotton saw prices plummet. The trading value of the US dollar sank.

US President Woodrow Wilson was intent on staying above the conflict. On 19 August, Wilson, whose beloved wife Ellen had died 13 days earlier, issued a statement to his melting-pot nation noting that its people were drawn "chiefly from the nations now at war". If Americans were to take sides, the divisions created would cause irreparable damage to the country's psyche, he warned. Instead America must occupy a studiously neutral position, "fit and free to do what is honest and disinterested and truly serviceable for the peace of the world".

Neiberg says that initially most Americans thought the war would be over quickly "or that it wouldn't touch American shores". They were supportive of Wilson's neutrality stance because it meant they retained the ability to trade freely within Europe. This was true in theory, but in practice, "to quote a German quip of the time, 'American neutrality spoke with a British accent'." The naval blockade established by the British at the start of the war prevented the sale of American goods to Germany or the other Central Powers, so these exports, including munitions, went to the UK and its allies.

Germany responded to the blockade with submarine warfare. In May 1915 the British liner *Lusitania*, returning to Liverpool from New York with 1,959 people aboard, was torpedoed by a U-boat off Ireland. Among the 1,198 killed were 128 American citizens. The attack provoked outrage in the US and England. (Germany justified it by saying the *Lusitania* had been transporting munitions. The Allies strenuously denied this for decades. It was in fact true, although the amount and type are still in dispute.)

A week after the sinking the US sent the German government the first of three official protest notes in which Wilson insisted upon the right of neutral citizens to travel by sea. This position put him at odds with his Secretary of State, William Jennings Bryan, who felt that the advent of submarine warfare meant the only way to keep American citizens safe was to ban them from overseas travel, and that if Wilson was going to chastise Germany he must do the same to Britain because it too had violated the rights of "neutrals". When Wilson sent his second note to Berlin, Bryan resigned.

Michael Neiberg is adamant that the sinking of the *Lusitania* "did not cause American entry into World War I no matter how many textbooks repeat that". But it was important in making the American people realise "they could not stay out of this war simply by ignoring it; they were going to have to figure out how they wanted to interact with and how they wanted to react with this war. And that's what really opened the debate in 1916 between people who were arguing for what became known as 'preparedness', that is, doing something to get the United States ready, and those people who argued for an even greater level of neutrality; people like William Jennings Bryan."

In fact 1916 was a year of many tensions, overt and hidden, domestic and international, affecting America. In April its relations with the British government came under increasing strain following Britain's merciless response to the Easter Uprising by Irish republicans. At the same time, relations with Germany eased a little after Berlin stopped targeting shipping in British waters. Then at the end of July came a disaster in New York Harbor that was initially believed to be an accident but was, in fact, German-sponsored sabotage.

Despite the *Lusitania* incident and subsequent less damaging U-boat attacks, the German and US governments had maintained diplomatic relations. But secretly the German Ambassador to the US, Count Johann Heinrich von Bernstorff, had been operating a propaganda and industrial espionage team since 1914. They'd had some small successes, but on 30 July 1916 Bernstorff's operatives pulled off a major coup.

The vast majority of all the armaments and munitions sold by America to the Entente Allies moved through a site called Black Tom Island in New Jersey, a short distance across the water from the Statue of Liberty. When the German-backed agents blew it up, they destroyed more than 950,000 kg of TNT, black powder, shrapnel and dynamite in a single strike. A baby and, it is thought, six adults died; hundreds of people were injured; and millions were terrified by an explosion heard as far away as Connecticut. (Not until 1939 would an investigatory commission find that it had indeed been German sabotage; the final restitution payment was made in 1979.)

But 1916 wasn't over yet. In December, Woodrow Wilson faced an election. With a campaign that confirmed his neutral stance and featured the catch-cry "He kept us out of the war", Wilson narrowly won a second presidential term. Neiberg says at this stage many Americans still felt that "supporting Britain and France through trade, through economics, through financial links, through volunteers going to Britain and France — and there were thousands of Americans who did that — was sufficient, that the United States didn't need to become involved in the war".

Wilson did see a role for his country in the conflict: not as a combatant, but as a peacemaker. First he made diplomatic overtures to the warring parties, urging them "on behalf of humanity" as well as neutral nations like his own, to work together towards a peaceful solution, with US mediation to aid the process. A month later, on 22 January 1917, he updated the US Senate on the reception to these overtures.

All parties, he said, had been responsive, the Central Powers generically so and the Entente Allies more specifically. All had given explicit reassurances that they did not want to crush their opponents; these reassurances, Wilson said, implied that the war must end in "peace without victory" because "Victory would mean peace forced upon the loser, a victor's terms imposed upon the vanquished. It would be accepted in humiliation, under duress, at intolerable sacrifice, and would leave a sting, a resentment, a bitter memory upon which terms of peace would rest, not permanently, but only as upon quicksand." They were prophetic words.

Unbeknownst to Wilson, just days beforehand German foreign minister Arthur Zimmermann had taken a bold step to minimise America's impact on Europe by attempting to drag it into war elsewhere. Via Ambassador Bernstorff, Zimmermann sent a coded telegram to the official German representative in Mexico, Heinrich von Eckhardt. He opened with the news that on 1 February Germany would be commencing unrestricted submarine warfare. In spite of this, he wrote, its government would try to get America to maintain neutrality. Then came the startling part. If America did enter the war against Germany, Eckhardt was to offer the Mexican president a deal: in exchange for taking arms against America, Germany would provide "generous financial support" to Mexico and help it recover the territory it had previously lost to the US in Texas, New Mexico and Arizona. Mexico was also to approach the Japanese in an attempt to get them on side.

Britain intercepted the telegram and decrypted it almost immediately. But in order to minimise the chances of the Germans realising their codes had been cracked, and to obtain maximum impact from the revelation, London held off telling the Americans for more than a month. Wilson finally learned about Zimmermann's message on 24 February and authorised its publication in American newspapers on 1 March. Five weeks later America declared war on Germany. This wasn't a move the president had to sell, says Neiberg. "Rather than Wilson trying to pull a reluctant nation into war, the American people had made a decision that they wanted the United States to get involved."

Nonetheless, Wilson was perfectly well aware that American strategic interests did not overlap perfectly with those of Britain and France, says Neiberg. Which is why when the United States did get involved in the war it did not sign the 1915 Treaty of London, which had bound Britain, France and Russia together, and didn't even call itself an ally, using the term "associated power" instead.

The other distinction important to Americans was the one between Germany's government and its people. Neiberg says right from the start of the war "the vast majority of Americans — including many second- and third-generation German-Americans — blamed the

German government. They didn't blame the German people, they blamed the regime." The speech Wilson gave on 2 April 1917 seeking approval from Congress to go to war made this distinction crystal clear. In a sense, Neiberg says, "the United States saw itself as liberating the German people from its own government."

At the end of May Wilson announced that he had selected General John Pershing to lead what would become the American Expeditionary Force. Pershing was in France by June and the following month submitted a report in which he asked for one million men to be available to fight by 1918, building up to three million "in order to win the war in 1919". This was an enormous leap from the total of 300,000 men, including soldiers, reserves and National Guard (many not mobilised) that the US Army could call on at the time. Those men who were available were equipped and trained for frontier protection, not trench warfare. No wonder, as Neiberg notes, it took the US a long time to mobilise: "The United States was not really a player on the Western Front until the spring of 1918."

But the war didn't stop to wait for the Americans. In Europe, France was fighting for its very survival with the full-blooded support of Britain and its Dominions along the Western Front. Meanwhile Russia, with some help from smaller allies Serbia and Romania, fought the German and Austro-Hungarian forces along the Eastern Front, which stretched over 1,600 km from the Black Sea to the Baltic.

The precise number of Russian casualties will probably never be known, but it was in the millions, and after two and a half years of suffering the Russian people had had enough.

In February 1917 the first Russian Revolution forced Tsar Nicholas II to abdicate. This revolution was the result of pressures that had been building for a long time. But, says Professor Margaret MacMillan, if the country had not been at war these pressures might have been resolved very differently. "Clearly huge changes were taking place in Russia. It was industrialising very fast, getting a growing middle class and a very rapidly growing working class, and it was going through the strains which so often accompany that rapid sort of development. It had an autocratic system which was badly out of touch and out of date which needed to make changes, and it very nearly had a revolution in 1905–1906 at the end of the Russo-Japanese War."

Even so, she says, without the First World War Russia might easily have undergone a more peaceful evolution. But the conflict illuminated the weaknesses of the Tsarist regime, which failed to cope with the demands of the war and became "increasingly corrupt and incompetent". The overthrow of Nicholas and the refusal of his brother Michael to replace him on the throne brought a sudden end to three centuries of dynastic Romanov rule. A provisional government began to rule but the new leaders made what MacMillan describes as "the fatal mistake" of deciding to stay in the deeply unpopular war.

Germany had a huge stake in the outcome of the upheavals inside Russia, because every piece of artillery, every army unit, every container of fuel it had to send to the Eastern Front caused an absence it felt on the Western Front. The Germans wanted to end the war on the Eastern Front, MacMillan says, so they could move troops back to the Western Front "and deal with Britain and France and their allies before the Americans came in". When it became clear that the February Revolution wasn't going to deliver the desired results, they took direct action.

Since the start of the war Germany had been keeping tabs on, and in many cases staying in contact with, would-be Russian revolutionaries who had been exiled under the Tsar. One of them was Vladimir Ilyich Lenin, who by 1917 was living in Zurich. Lenin sent out feelers to the German Ambassador asking if he and a group of supporters would be permitted to travel through Germany en route to Russia. Berlin said yes even after Lenin imposed conditions, including anonymity for all. The German government supplied a sealed carriage and used police and military personnel to seal off station platforms when the train stopped along the way. Lenin and his party were delivered to the Baltic port of Sassnitz, where they boarded a steamer for the short trip to Sweden, thence by train to Petrograd.

The Germans, says MacMillan, were hoping that Lenin would "spread the infection of Bolshevism and thereby help to knock Russia out of the war, which is in fact what happened". Lenin's message to demoralised Russians was, she says, brilliantly simple and effective: "Peace, Bread and Land". In October 1917 the Bolsheviks seized power in a coup. One of their first official acts was to publish peace proposals. Fighting on the Eastern Front ended shortly afterwards and peace negotiations with Germany began at Brest-Litovsk on 22 December.

Supposedly the peace treaty was to be negotiated without reparations or annexations, but under the version finally signed in March, Russia gave up the Ukraine, Finland and more: about one million square kilometres in total, home to 50 million people. Germany, says MacMillan, walked away with control over much-needed raw material and "forced the Bolsheviks to hand over a good deal of gold, which went into the German war effort".

It might initially seem bizarre that having secured these advantages Germany kept advancing to the east. But the goal was something it desperately needed: oil, specifically the enormous oil reserves around Baku on the Caspian Sea. In fact, while Germany pulled around a million troops out of Russia and sent them to fight on the Western Front, a million stayed behind to occupy the Ukraine and enforce the Brest-Litovsk Treaty. MacMillan says the "desperate gamble" of maintaining such a large presence in the east was driven in part by the effectiveness of the British naval blockade in preventing Germany from getting fuel and other vital supplies including food.

On the Western Front, meanwhile, the US troops had finally arrived. Emphasising their separateness from the Entente Allies, Wilson and Pershing strongly opposed the idea of splitting the US troops up and weaving them into existing units. "The argument the French and British made was that because the soldiers from the United States were so untested and so new to modern warfare, they could best be used under British and French commanders," explains Neiberg. Wilson and Pershing were adamant that such "amalgamation" was not acceptable.

The debate continues over what effect the American presence had. Professor Robin Prior, author of six books on the First World War, says if the fighting had dragged on the Americans would have made an enormous difference. "If the war had gone on into 1919 they would have had the largest army on the Western Front. General Pershing would have headed that army and he wanted to go on and occupy Berlin, which none of the other generals did. So if the war had lasted longer the American manpower would have been absolutely crucial. But in 1918 it's mainly the British Army that defeats the Germans. The Americans think they won the war in 1918; I think they made a contribution but it was more a financial and resources contribution than a military one."

Michael Neiberg has a different take. For him the sheer size of the American force had an immediate impact. In 1918, "despite the German navy's claim that it could sink the transport ships, the United States lands on average almost 20,000 men per day in France and there's simply nothing that a war-ravaged, influenza-ravaged Germany can do to stop that. What that gives the Allies is the opportunity to move units around. It allows the Allies to build more solid elastic defences in key parts of the line." In short, he says, it increased the strategic options available to French general Ferdinand Foch, who was given overall command of the Allied forces that April.

But Prior argues that the Americans didn't get their own sector of the Western Front until August 1918, by which time the Allies had already made all-important progress. "Numbers don't count for much in the First World War; if you have more men that just means more casualties. In 1916 and 1917 the Allies had more men and it got them nowhere." He acknowledges that as the European summer drew to a close in 1918 the Allies maintained a numerical advantage thanks to successful but costly German advances. "From March to July the Germans had attacked on the Western Front and they'd lost something around a million men, so when the Allies moved to a counter-attack they were already facing a weakened German army."

But, he says, it was a different kind of superiority that made all the difference. "There was a slow evolution on the Western Front, with the Allies getting technologically better and better," says Prior. "By 1918 they can take out the German guns without firing a preliminary bombardment. In previous battles you'd had to fire an enormous bombardment to soften up the enemy positions. The bombardments at the Somme lasted for seven or eight days, and of course that gave the enemy a warning that you were going to attack." But by the time of the Battle of Amiens in August 1918, "they have located the position of every German gun by a technique called sound-ranging, so they don't have to fire a preliminary bombardment; at zero-hour their guns open fire and take out the entire German artillery on that part of the front. This is a marvellous technological breakthrough in which a South Australian, Lawrence Bragg, played a major role."

That wasn't the only technological advantage the Allies enjoyed. "They had portable machine guns, Lewis guns, they had rifle grenades, they had trench mortars. They've got 500 tanks at the Battle of Amiens; the Germans

I think only ever produced seven tanks. All of that means the Germans and their rather rudimentary fortifications are completely overrun: there's an advance of about nine miles on the first day, which doesn't sound much but in Western Front terms it's cosmic."

General Erich Ludendorff, who was running Germany's strategy on the Western Front, described his side's failure at Amiens as "the black day of the German army". The Germans' remaining hope, says Prior, was the Hindenburg Line, a formidable defensive system of trenches, tunnels and pillbox-mounted machine guns that the Allies had been unable to penetrate the previous year. This time, "instead of using tricky methods, they just used brute force". By this point the British munitions industry was the largest in the world, "so guns can fire a million shells in 24 hours; nothing can withstand that sort of firepower." In a two-part attack that began on 18 September led by Australian and US troops, the line was broken.

Despite this devastating blow, German troops continued advancing on the Baku oilfields in Eastern Europe into October. They were, says Prior, intent on war aims that foreshadowed their strategy in World War II:

"advancing as far into Russia, conquering as much territory and getting hold of as much oil as they possibly could".

During this period the erratic Ludendorff, realising that the war was lost, demanded Germany begin armistice negotiations, only to change his mind weeks later. Beginning to understand what would be extracted from Germany in the armistice, he demanded that Germany fight on. On 26 October, when it became clear this was not going to happen, Kaiser Wilhelm II accepted Ludendorff's resignation.

In voluntary exile in Sweden Ludendorff wrote at length about how victory had been snatched from him and his wonderful soldiers because they had been "stabbed in the back" by left-wingers on the home front. This is self-serving nonsense, say our historians. "The myth is that the Germans were stabbed in the back," says Prior, "but while all this was going on the Allies were actually stabbing them in the front."

As we saw in Chapter 7, there certainly was agitation within Germany, but, says Margaret MacMillan, that is not why it lost the war. "Germany lost fairly and squarely on the battlefields, but the German people were getting increasingly impatient with the privations under which they were living; the German government was in fact by this point more or less a military dictatorship and was not really looking after the civilians that well. They didn't have proper rationing and Germans were going very, very short of a number of things."

It wasn't just civilians who no longer bought the line that this was a war Germany had to keep on fighting. Many in the military, too, had lost faith. "You were beginning to get discontent in parts of the army," MacMillan says, "and particularly in the navy, which had been the great pride and joy of the Kaiser and his old regime but had basically been sitting in port for much of the time." Two days after Ludendorff stepped down, with Germany already in talks with the Allies about how an armistice might be achieved, German Naval Command decided to launch a last-ditch attack on the British fleet without the knowledge of the German Chancellor. Understanding this to be a suicide mission, German sailors began to mutiny. Despite more than 1,000 being arrested, within a week the uprising had spread across the country from the naval base at Kiel to cities including Hamburg, Bremen and Munich. In response, the Socialist members of parliament declared Germany to be a republic on 9 November. Two days later the war was over.

So, the Allies' technological advances, the privations caused by Germany's inability to provide basic supplies to its people, and its persistence in pushing eastwards when resources were badly needed elsewhere all played a part. So too did the US presence, says Neiberg, despite the fact that the American Expeditionary Force was only in major combat operations for five months. Its arrival in Europe "makes it obvious to the Germans that any war they fight in 1919 they're going to fight under far less advantageous circumstances than they had fought in 1918 or 1917".

He says that this was one of the catalysts that led Germans to seek an armistice. "Could the Allies have won the war without the Americans? Probably. But I think once the Americans make the decision to mobilise fully, to engage fully, to deploy an army to the continent of Europe and to continue to sustain and support that army, then the odds of Germany winning reduce to almost zero. And the German senior leadership understood that."

Margaret MacMillan agrees. "Most people were expecting the fighting to go on into 1919. The German military knew that by 1919 they would be confronting this huge boost to Allied manpower, and I think this was something that helped to undermine German morale."

In the first three years of the war the Allies had drawn on resources from the vast empires of Britain and France, which Germany couldn't begin to match. The huge US-supplied influx of wealth and manpower in 1918 was the death-knell: Germany was "simply exhausted". The guns fell silent. The war was over.

EPILOGUE

It is easier to make war than peace.

> — Georges Clemenceau, French Prime Minister,
> presiding over the Paris Peace Conference, 20 July 1919

Four years, that's all. The Great War occupied just four of the five and a half thousand years of recorded human history, but it changed so much.

Its importance was obvious even while it was still going on. On 10 September 1918, two months and thousands of casualties before the armistice, US war historian Robert Matteson Johnston sought a meeting with the influential British war correspondent Charles à Court Repington (critic of the war's "side-shows"). Among other things they discussed how the war ought to be known.

Repington noted in his diary, "I said that we called it now The War, but that this could not last. The Napoleonic

War was The Great War. To call it The German War was too much flattery for the Boche. I suggested The World War as a shade better title, and finally we mutually agreed to call it The First World War in order to prevent the millennium folk from forgetting that the history of the world was the history of war."

We are the millennium folk he was referring to. We haven't forgotten, although we often struggle to get our minds around the scale of the devastation. There are no firm numbers on the war's dead, injured and missing. We do, however, have well-informed estimates, and they stretch our understanding to the limit.

It is believed 8,500,000 troops died, either in action or from injuries or disease. But it wasn't just soldiers and sailors and airmen who paid the price. At least as many civilians — and perhaps millions more — died as a direct result of the war, including those who starved to death. A significant part of the reason these are best guesses is the influenza pandemic that began in the US and was unwittingly brought to France by American troops. It overlapped with the last few months of the war and continued into 1919, killing more than 25 million people. Death on such scale made accurate record-keeping impossible.

The flu pandemic was still sweeping Europe when the Paris Peace Conference was taking place at Versailles; US President Woodrow Wilson became bedridden with the illness during vital parts of the negotiations. Wilson's temporary absence was no doubt a blessed relief to outspoken 78-year-old French Prime Minister Georges Clemenceau. The American had arrived at the conference bearing his famous Fourteen Point plan, prompting Clemenceau's exclamation, "The good Lord had only 10!"

Much discussion has focused on these talks and how much the conditions imposed upon Germany in the resulting Treaty of Versailles fed into the Second World War. Certainly Clemenceau was intent on harsh punishment for France's aggressive neighbour. He already held a grudge dating back four decades to the Franco-Prussian War, and France had suffered greatly in this latest war, with almost one in four of the young men who went to fight being killed, millions more maimed, and homes and farms by the millions destroyed.

British Prime Minister David Lloyd George tried to argue for a more moderate approach, and at least once he and Clemenceau came close to blows. Clemenceau himself described how "Wilson had to interpose between us with outstretched arms, saying pleasantly, 'Well, well! I have never come across two such unreasonable men!'" As Michael Neiberg says, the key question was: "Once you've won the war, what do you then want the post-war world to look like? And on that there was even more disagreement than there had been about wartime policy."

In Professor Margaret MacMillan's view, "The First World War doesn't lead directly to the Second World War, but it makes possible the conditions which help to produce a second world war." In the aftermath of Versailles, she says, Germans felt a deep sense of resentment, believing "that they didn't really lose the war and the treaty was unfair. But there are 20 years between the end of the First World War and the outbreak of the Second. You cannot say that the First World War led directly to the Second World War. Lots happened in between and lots of decisions were made or not made."

For instance, she says, "Among the other factors leading to the Second World War was Hitler getting into power, which didn't have to happen — you had stupid German elites who thought they could use him. And of course there was the Great Depression, which tended to push people down the road of looking for more radical solutions. We have to look at the complexity of history, not look for really simple connections between events that are often widely separated by time."

Professor Robin Prior agrees. "One war at a time. The problem with the First World War is it's overshadowed by the Second World War. But it has a right to exist. If Germany had won it you would have had a Europe dominated by authoritarian militarism and that would have been in the interests of no one, certainly not France, not the British Empire, not the Dominions. This autocratic militarism had to be stopped, and it was a better world when it was," he says.

Michael Neiberg sees things differently, arguing that in some ways it is helpful to view the two wars as a single entity: "almost a second Thirty Years' War". He has said that while he sometimes jokes he can trace any subsequent event back to World War I, its influence cannot be overstated: "It's impossible for me to see how the Second World War, the Holocaust, the Cold War, a globally engaged United States, and decolonisation could have happened without it."

MacMillan says the war certainly set the stage for changes unlikely to have occurred if peace had prevailed.

"We'll never know, but I think it's highly unlikely that the Bolsheviks, a tiny little splinter group, most of whose leaders were in exile or in jail, could have seized power if it hadn't been for the disruption caused by the war. They seized power and most people thought they'd be gone in a week, and of course they lasted till the end of the 1980s. And I think you probably wouldn't have got the rise of these heavily militarised radical nationalist parties that you got in Germany and places like Hungary and Italy without the brutalisation caused to society by the First World War."

Neiberg points to specific countries such as Syria, whose ruling family got its power as a result of the war, as well as to large-scale changes that resulted from the post-war collapse of the various empires. He says that the decades that followed — the 1930s, when fascism, democracy and communism were pitted against one another; the Cold War of the 1950s; and power struggles going on right now in the Middle East — have all been attempts to fill the vacuum left by the collapse of the colonial powers.

For writer Peter Hitchens, "the outbreak of war in 1939 was the final blow to anybody who'd believed in

1914 that this had been a war for civilisation, let alone a war to end war. From then on, the reputation of that war has sunk and sunk and sunk and nobody can really find a seriously good word to say for it."

This view comes as no surprise to Professor Jay Winter, author of books including *The Experience of World War I* and *Remembering War: The Great War Between History and Memory in the 20th Century*. "In the Anglo-Saxon world (very different from other countries), there has been a progressive story about futility which varies according to country and according to generation. It's very difficult to persuade British people, young and old, that there was a point, a reason for the casualties of the Great War," he says. "The way the poet Ted Hughes put it was that the Great War was 'defeat around whose neck someone hung a victory medal'."

Other countries see it according to their own experiences. "In France there were one million uninvited guests in the north of the country who had to be expelled, so the First World War is not futile in French memory. In Germany the loss of the war makes it an embarrassment, a difficulty and … a subject not really touched until recent years."

Views might prevail across a culture but they aren't being handed down from on high, he says. "Every nation carries its own stories based in the way ordinary people talk over the dinner table or the breakfast table, much more than what the state wants them to think or what historians do. Most of the remembrance of the First World War is based in family stories. Historians are really fellow travellers in an extraordinary conversation going on around the world about what happened between 1914 and 1918. We who write about this are really very marginal players; it's families who tell stories and who pass them on from generation to generation."

It takes conscious effort to honour those who came before and remember their lives. "Stories fade away; they only stay alive because people take the time and the effort and the money to keep them alive. That's why Australian pilgrimage to Gallipoli is so important," says Winter.

Even now, he maintains, there is nothing to match the Great War in terms of its "sacred power". "There was an extraordinary moment when Australian soldiers were re-buried at Fromelles in 2010 after their remains had been identified. The families came over and they chose for some of the gravestones the epigram 'Once I was lost and now I'm found' from the hymn 'Amazing Grace'. It was extraordinarily powerful. If you had seen the ceremony and the tears that it evoked in just about everybody, you would understand how the First World War is still alive and will take an awfully long time to fade away."

APPENDIX

About the historians

William Altman

A Latin and world history teacher based in Virginia, USA, and the author of books including:

Friedrich Wilhelm Nietzsche: The Philosopher of the Second Reich
(Lexington Books, 2012)

Martin Heidegger and the First World War (Lexington Books,
2012)

Joan Beaumont

Professor of History, Strategic and Defence Studies Centre, ANU College of Asia and the Pacific, and author of publications including:

Broken Nation: Australians in the Great War (Allen & Unwin,
2013)

Scott Bennett

Professor of History, Georgian Court University, and author/editor of:

Radical Pacifism: The War Resisters League and Gandhian Nonviolence in America, 1915–1963 (Syracuse University Press, 2003)

Army GI, Pacifist CO: The World War II Letters of Frank and Albert Dietrich (ed.) (Fordham University Press, 2005)

Robert Bollard

Lecturer in History, School of Social Sciences and Psychology, Victoria University, and author of:

In the Shadow of Gallipoli: The Hidden History of Australia in World War I (New South Books, 2013)

Harvey Broadbent

Senior Research Fellow in Modern History at Macquarie University, directing a research project centred on the Turkish military archives and the Gallipoli campaign, and author of books including:

Gallipoli: The Fatal Shore (Penguin, 2009)

Ute Daniel

Professor of History at the Technical University of Braunschweig, and author of books including:

The War from Within: German Women in the First World War (Berg
Publishers, 1997)

Santanu Das

Reader in English Literature, King's College London, and author/
editor of books including:

Touch and Intimacy in First World War Literature (Cambridge
University Press, 2006)

The Cambridge Companion to the Poetry of the First World War (ed.)
(Cambridge University Press, 2013)

Race, Empire and First World War Writing (ed.) (Cambridge
University Press, 2014)

Hugo Drochon

Postdoctoral Research Fellow at Cambridge University specialising
in modern continental political thought, in particular the political
thought of Friedrich Nietzsche.

Ann-Marie Einhaus

Lecturer in Modern and Contemporary Literature, Northumbria
University, and author/editor of books including:

The Penguin Book of First World War Stories (co-ed. with Barbara
Korte) (Penguin, 2007)

The Short Story and the First World War (Cambridge University
Press, 2013)

Ashley Ekins

Head of the Military History section of the Australian War
Memorial and author/co-author of two of the nine volumes in the
Official History of Australian Involvement in Southeast Asian
Conflicts 1948–1975. His other books include:

*1918, Year of Victory: The End of the Great War and the Shaping of
History* (ed.) (Exisle Publishing, 2010)

War Wounds: Medicine and the Trauma of Conflict (co-ed. with
Elizabeth Stewart) (Exisle Publishing, 2011)

Gallipoli: A Ridge Too Far (ed.) (Exisle Publishing, 2013)

Marvin B. Fried

Teacher of the history of the First World War and 20th-century
international history at the London School of Economics, and
author of:

Austro-Hungarian War Aims in the Balkans During World War I
(Palgrave Macmillan, 2014)

David Grant

Author of 13 books including:

*Field Punishment No 1: Archibald Baxter, Mark Briggs and New
    Zealand's Anti-Militarist Tradition* (Steele Roberts, 2008)
*A Question of Faith: A History of the New Zealand Christian Pacifist
    Society* (Philip Garside, 2013)

Paul Ham

Historian and author of books including:

Kokoda (HarperCollins, 2004)

Sandakan (Random House, 2011)

1914: The Year the World Ended (William Heinemann, 2013)

Gerhard Hirschfeld

Professor of History at the Historical Institute of the University of
Stuttgart, and author of books including:

Scorched Earth: The Germans on the Somme 1914–1918 (with G.
    Krumeich and I. Renz) (Pen & Sword Military, 2009)
Brill's Encyclopedia of the First World War (co-ed. with
    G. Krumeich and I. Renz) (Brill, 2012)

Peter Hitchens

Journalist and author of nine books including:

The Rage Against God (Continuum, 2010)

Bernd Hüppauf

Professor Emeritus of German Literature and Literary Theory, New York University, and the author/editor of many books, including:

War, Violence and the Modern Condition (ed.) (De Gruyter, 2010)

Philip Jenkins

Distinguished Professor of History, Baylor University, and author of more than 20 books, including:

The Great and Holy War: How World War I Became a Religious Crusade (HarperOne, 2014)

Edgar Jones

Professor of the History of Medicine and Psychiatry at the Institute of Psychiatry, King's College London, and the author of:

Shell Shock to PTSD: Military Psychiatry from 1900 to the Gulf War (with S. Wessely) (Hove, 2005)

John W. Langdon

Professor of History at Le Moyne College, and author of many books, including:

July 1914: The Long Debate 1918–1990 (Berg Publishers, 1991)

Joseph Loconte

Associate Professor of History at The King's College, New York City, and author of the forthcoming *A Hobbit, a Wardrobe and a Great War: How C.S. Lewis and J.R.R. Tolkien Rediscovered Faith, Friendship and Heroism in the Cataclysm of 1914–18*. His other books include:

The End of Illusions: Religious Leaders Confront Hitler's Gathering Storm (Rowman & Littlefield, 2004)

Margaret MacMillan

The Warden of St Antony's College and Professor of International History at the University of Oxford; she is the author of books, including:

Paris 1919: Six Months that Changed the World (Random House, 2002)

The War that Ended Peace: The Road to 1914 (Profile Books, 2014)

Emily Mayhew

Research Associate in the Centre for Co-curricular Studies, Imperial College, London, an Examiner at the Imperial College School of Medicine and the author of:

Wounded: The Long Journey Home from the Great War (Vintage, 2014; first published as *Wounded: From Battlefield to Blighty, 1914–1918*, The Bodley Head, 2013)

Annika Mombauer

Senior Lecturer in Modern European History at the Open University UK, and author of books including:

Helmuth von Moltke and the Origins of the First World War
   (Cambridge University Press, 2001)

The Origins of the First World War: Controversies and Consensus
   (Longman, 2002)

The Kaiser: New Research on Wilhelm II's Role in Imperial Germany
   (Cambridge University Press, 2010)

Kerry Neale

Assistant Curator at the Australian War Memorial and PhD candidate, focusing on the medical responses to facially disfigured soldiers during World War I, in her thesis "Without the Faces of Men".

Michael S. Neiberg

Professor of History, Department of National Security and Strategy at the US Army War College, and author of books including:

Fighting the Great War: A Global History (Harvard University
   Press, 2006)

Dance of the Furies: Europe and the Outbreak of World War I
   (Harvard University Press, 2011)

Gary Oakley

Indigenous Liaison Officer at the Australian War Memorial, and National President of the Aboriginal and Torres Strait Islander Veterans and Services Association.

Bobbie Oliver

Associate Professor of History, Department of Social Sciences and International Studies at Curtin University, and author of books including:

War and Peace in Western Australia (University of Western
   Australia, 1995)

*Peacemongers: Conscientious Objectors to Military Service in
   Australia, 1911–1945* (Fremantle Press, 1997)

Cyril Pearce

Senior Lecturer (Retired) and Visiting Fellow at Leeds University, creator of a database of conscientious objectors in Britain, and author of the forthcoming *Communities of Resistance: Patterns of Dissent in Britain During the First World War*. His other books include:

*Comrades in Conscience: The Story of an English Community's
   Opposition to the Great War* (Francis Boutle, 2001)

William Philpott

Professor of the History of Warfare, Department of War Studies, King's College London, and author of books including:

Anglo-French Relations and Strategy on the Western Front, 1914–1918 (Macmillan, 1996)

The Palgrave Concise Historical Atlas of the First World War (with Matthew Hughes) (Palgrave Macmillan, 2005)

Bloody Victory: The Sacrifice on the Somme and the Making of the Twentieth Century (Little, Brown, July 2009)

Attrition: Fighting the First World War (Little, Brown, 2014)

Robin Prior

Visiting Professorial Fellow, School of History and Politics at the University of Adelaide, and author of books including:

Command on the Western Front: The Military Career of General Sir Henry Rawlinson 1914–1918 (Blackwell, 1992)

Passchendaele: The Untold Story (with Trevor Wilson) (Yale University Press, 1996)

The First World War (Cassell, 1999)

The Somme (with Trevor Wilson) (Yale University Press, 2005)

Gallipoli: The End of the Myth (Yale University Press / University of New South Wales Press, 2009)

Eugene Rogan

Associate Professor of the Modern History of the Middle East, Faculty of Oriental Studies, University of Oxford, and author of books including:

The Arabs: A History (Basic Books, 2009)

The Fall of the Ottomans: The Great War in the Middle East (Allen Lane, 2015)

Philippa Scarlett

Author of *Aboriginal and Torres Strait Islander Volunteers for the AIF: The Indigenous Response to World War One* (Indigenous Histories, 2012).

Gary Sheffield

Professor of War Studies at the University of Wolverhampton, and author of many books, including:

Forgotten Victory: The First World War — Myths and Realities (Headline, 2001)

The Somme: A New History (Cassell, 2004)

The Chief: Douglas Haig and the British Army (Aurum Press, 2011)

Command and Morale: The British Army on the Western Front 1914–1918 (Pen & Sword Military, 2014)

Vincent Sherry

Howard Nemerov Professor in the Humanities, Professor of English, Washington University in St Louis, and author/editor of books including:

The Great War and the Language of Modernism (Oxford University
Press, 2003)

The Cambridge Companion to the Literature of the First World War
(ed.) (Cambridge University Press, 2005)

Gajendra Singh

Arts and Humanities Research Council Early Career Fellow in the Department of Continuing Education, Kellogg College, University of Oxford, and the author of:

*The Testimonies of Indian Soldiers and the Two World Wars: Between
Self and Sepoy* (Bloomsbury, 2014)

Christina Spittel

Lecturer in English, University of New South Wales, currently completing a book on the treatment of the First World War in Australian novels.

Peter Stanley

Research Professor at the Australian Centre for the Study of Armed Conflict and Society, University of New South Wales and author of 25 books, including:

Australians at War, 1885–1972: Photographs from the Collection of the Australian War Memorial (with Michael McKernan) (William Collins 1984)

A Stout Pair of Boots: A Guide to Exploring Australia's Battlefields (Allen & Unwin, 2008)

Bad Characters: Sex, Crime, Mutiny, Murder and the Australian Imperial Force (Pier 9, 2010)

Digger Smith and Australia's Great War (Pier 9, 2011)

Claudia Sternberg

Senior Lecturer in Cultural Studies and, a member of the Legacies of War Centenary project at the University of Leeds, and author of books including:

Der Erste Weltkrieg und die Mediendiskurse der Erinnerung in Grossbritannien: Autobiografie, Roman, Film, 1919–1999 (*The First World War in Britain and the Media Discourses of Memory: Autobiography, Novel, Film, 1919–1999*) (with B. Korte and R. Schneider) (Königshausen & Neumann, 2004)

Sir Hew Strachan

Chichele Professor of the History of War, All Souls College, University of Oxford, and author of many books, including:

The Oxford Illustrated History of the First World War (Oxford University Press, first published 1998, updated 2014)

The First World War: A New History (Simon & Schuster, first published 2003, updated 2014)

The First World War in Africa (Oxford University Press, 2014)

Salim Tamari

Director of the Institute of Palestine Studies and Adjunct Professor at the Center for Contemporary Arab Studies, Georgetown University, Washington, DC, and author of books including:

Ihsan's War: The Intimate Life of an Ottoman Soldier (Institute for Palestine Studies, 2008)

Year of the Locust: A Soldier's Diary and the Erasure of Palestine's Ottoman Past (University of California Press, 2011)

Mesut Uyar

Ottoman Fellow, Associate Professor of History, Australian Centre for the Study of Armed Conflict and Society at the University of New South Wales, Canberra, and author of books including:

A Military History of the Turks: From Osman to Ataturk (with
 Edward J. Erickson) (Praeger, 2009)

Christine Winter

Senior Research Fellow in the Department of History, University
of Sydney, Honorary Research Senior Fellow at the University of
Queensland, and author of books including:

Looking After One's Own: The Rise of Nationalist — and the Politics
 of the Neuendettelsauer Mission in Australia, New Guinea and
 Germany (1921–1933) (Peter Lang, 2012)

Jay Winter

Charles J. Stille Professor of History at Yale University, and author
of numerous books, including:

The Experience of World War I (Oxford University Press, 1988)

Sites of Memory, Sites of Mourning: The Great War in European
 Cultural History (Cambridge University Press, 1999)

Remembering War: The Great War Between History and Memory in
 the 20th Century (Yale University Press, 2006)

Xu Guoqi

Professor of History at the University of Hong Kong, and author
of books including:

China and the Great War: China's Pursuit of a New National Identity and Internationalization (Cambridge University Press, 2005)

Strangers on the Western Front: Chinese Workers in the Great War (Harvard University Press, 2011)

ABC RN's radio series *The Great War: Memory, Perceptions and 10 Contested Questions* is also available as an audiobook on USB from ABC Audio. Featuring the complete nine hours of content, the USB is available from ABC Shops, online and in bookstores.